# ICE CREAM
## ADVENTURES

MORE THAN *100* DELICIOUSLY
DIFFERENT RECIPES

## STEF FERRARI

FOUNDER OF HAY ROSIE CRAFT ICE CREAM COMPANY

PHOTOGRAPHS BY TINA RUPP
FOREWORD BY PATRICK RUE OF THE BRUERY

RODALE

# RODALE *wellness*

*Live happy. Be healthy. Get inspired.*

Sign up today to get exclusive access to our authors, exclusive bonuses,
and the most authoritative, useful, and cutting-edge information on health,
wellness, fitness, and living your life to the fullest.

**Visit us online at RodaleWellness.com**
**Join us at RodaleWellness.com/Join**

Rodale books may be purchased for business or promotional use or for special sales.
For information, please write to:
Special Markets Department, Rodale Inc., 733 Third Avenue, New York, NY 10017

Printed in the United States of America
Rodale Inc. makes every effort to use acid-free ♾, recycled paper ♻.

Illustration Credits: Recurring ice cream cone from Karma3/Shutterstock
and recurring ice cream truck from Johavel/Shutterstock

Food Styling by Lisa Homa
Prop Styling by Stephanie Hanes
Book design by Rae Ann Spitzenberger

Library of Congress Cataloging-in-Publication Data is on file with the publisher.

ISBN 978–1–62336–672–8   hardcover

Distributed to the trade by Macmillan

2  4  6  8  10  9  7  5  3  1   hardcover

Follow us @RodaleBooks on 🐦 📘 📌 📷

We inspire and enable people to improve their lives and the world around them.
**rodalewellness.com**

FOR HEATHER & AVA

May every day be full of mother-daughter adventures.
The ice cream is optional but always advised.

# CONTENTS

# FOREWORD

The first time Stef told me she was going into the ice cream business, I thought she was a bit nuts. Stef is a beer expert, and I could clearly see her bright future in craft beer lined up. No, she wanted to get into ice cream. The first time I tasted her ice cream, I understood. Ice cream is where she has chosen to make her mark, and I am grateful she did. Before I get ahead of myself, let me back up and tell you how I know Stef.

I vividly remember the first time I met Stef. In early 2009, a very young yet confident Stef Ferrari arrives promptly for her interview at my brewery. She was likely a bit surprised to find herself in a rundown industrial complex in Orange County, California. At the time, the Bruery's Tasting Room consisted of homemade/Ikea furniture and an amateurish kegerator made by yours truly, surrounded by antique brewing equipment. The part that brought Stef to us was our unusual yet delicious, flavor-driven beers. Such examples of the beers of that time were an autumn beer with yams, a spring beer with Thai basil, sour beer aged with fruit in wine barrels.

A recent transplant from Connecticut, she conquered an interview for the Tasting Room manager position. This is a role my wife Rachel and I were particularly excited to fill. We had spent the last few months running the Tasting Room ourselves while doing everything else that running a brewery required, so we were tired by the time Stef showed up. It was truly a start-up, with about four co-workers at that time, one of which was my yellow lab Barley. I was so impressed by Stef's strong motor and an entrepreneurial spirit. She was filled with ideas on how to offer an amazing experience to our customers and on flavors we could incorporate into our beers. Being in a rundown industrial complex wasn't an issue for her. If anything, it made the experience more authentic, as innovation rarely comes from places in polished shopping centers. It was about the excitement of the beers made in this place.

Stef has an essential trait of a successful culinary entrepreneur: a strong sense of innovation when it comes to flavor. This skill is the ability to imagine all of the world's possible ingredients, textures, and temperatures and being able to translate that into a harmonious, delicious experience that is often unexpected and thought provoking. The most innovative in the culinary world use their medium as a way of expressing flavor rather than being bound by the rules of their culinary tradition. The less innovative have a steep hill to climb. There are many stories of a chef following tried-and-true recipes to find mediocrity; where a brewer goes after the traditional approach and makes an unremarkable portfolio of beers similar to 99 percent of everything else on the shelf. Perhaps the most atrocious would be an ice cream maker trying to break into the market with plain vanilla ice cream. Stef is a master of flavor, inspired by the many delicious ingredients and culinary traditions of the world and bringing that to ice cream. A great example of this is her recipe for Cacio e Pepe Ice Cream (page 83)—when's the last time you had savory ice cream on pasta? You'll wonder how you've gone your whole life without it.

While innovation is necessary to creating something new, quality must also play a key role. After all, originality is only successful if it's delicious! While at the Bruery, it was clear that quality was important for Stef in everything she did. Her commitment to quality of the ingredients in the ice cream and the processes was particularly impressive. She purchased milk directly from the farm, pasteurizing it herself. She made cookie dough, toffee, popcorn, sauces, and countless other toppings herself. Great expense went into finding the best fennel pollen, the most aromatic lavender to use in her creations. Everything that went into the ice cream was made or chosen with painstaking effort and love. It had to be the best...and it is. A great example of this is her Barnburner ice cream sandwich on page 181. (OMG, you gotta try it, but skip breakfast that day!)

To me, this book is all about how a flavor approach can make anything we eat more delicious and exciting. It's about what happens when the stars align—a motor, a sense of flavor, a commitment to quality, and of course, a very strong sense of adventure. Perhaps it'll light a fire in you to create something uniquely delicious!

*PATRICK RUE*
*CEO & Founder*
*The Bruery*

# MY LOVE LETTER TO ICE CREAM

I dream of ice cream—in my daydreams, during deep REM sleep, and quite often while I should be doing other things. I am constantly wishing I was somewhere with scoops of that sweet and creamy, frozen form of happiness. But I can't be blamed; it's in my DNA. My mother, Rosie, introduced me to the as-yet-unmatched elation of eating an ice cream cone when I was very young, and it quickly became our go-to bonding activity. Some of our most pivotal moments have taken place over a shared cone of butter pecan or raspberry chocolate truffle at our favorite farms in Connecticut, where I was raised.

For me, it's never been hard to explain the appeal; ice cream has always had my respect. Enjoying it is an activity rarely carried out alone or idly. It's not a cookie. It's not a bag of chips. It can't be stolen from a cabinet, perfunctorily plunked into a lunchbox on your way out the door.

By nature, eating ice cream requires planning, foresight. It demands certain conditions that can't be created on the fly. That's what makes it share-worthy. If you're going to go through the trouble of visiting the scoop shop, chances are you're probably going to bring along a buddy. You're going to stand in line together and talk about flavors you'd like to try. The ones you think you'll get or the ones you've had in the past. Maybe you'll consider sharing a sundae or debate whether to have sprinkles or fudge sauce or whipped cream. Once you're served, you'll probably trade opinions on how or why it's so good—the discussion being integral to the overall ritual.

And because of this obligation to create a conducive environment, eating ice cream is more likely to be timeless, memorable—a special event, often associated with feelings or experiences, good times or bad. Maybe you plowed through a pint of cookie dough the first time you were dumped. And maybe that same flavor was there to help you celebrate scoring a new job.

Ice cream is the center of attention. Obtaining it is often the objective of an outing, and its demanding nature persists because there's simply no way to passively consume a scoop. From the moment you start eating, it immediately begins its metamorphosis—the first bites firm and frozen, the final nearing a liquid state.

It's a tenuous process to negotiate, a high-stakes situation from start to finish: to expertly lick in an effective pattern, to strategize which sides to attack while it slowly but steadily threatens to deteriorate should it not receive proper attention. When it's displeased with your performance, it starts spitefully ceding chocolate chips or chunks of fruit, jam, and caramel, dripping in dissent, aggrieved by your inadequate assiduity.

It's needy and fickle. It's basically your crazy ex. It doesn't like you to look away, it doesn't have time or tolerance for your Instagramming, and it definitely doesn't defer to your iPhone.

In small ways, ice cream has made me a better person and a better friend. I find that the older I get, the more scatterbrained I become, my focus fractured by the frenzy of the day-to-day. But ice cream just won't have it. It grabs you by the hand and *forces* you to slow down and be present, to spend time with it and the people in front of you, to take a moment and just enjoy. The happiness is all in your hands, and ice cream reminds you that the moment won't last for very long.

Ice cream is a great equalizer. Seriously, have you ever considered how ridiculous we all look eating an ice cream cone? Attempting to keep up with a melting mass on a hot day, chasing a cone in circles with all the familiar maneuvers—the pivot, the swivel, the tongue stretched, the head in full tilt—it's a socially acceptable exercise in absurdity, bringing even the toughest and most hard-nosed headfirst into a drip-defying fury.

And when you submit entirely and yield your full attention, you'd be hard-pressed to find a more satisfying, delicious, and memorable reward. What's not to love?

And while ice cream has always maintained the top slot on my list of things I love to eat, I am also a robust enjoyer of all things edible and an observer of food culture in general. Like most Italian Americans, I come from a family that probably couldn't have produced an heir with any other predilection. Yes, my nonni does make *the* world's greatest dish of handmade pasta (sorry, everyone else's grandmother—it's an indisputable fact), so it's no wonder that I'm predisposed to this passion.

I consider myself one of the luckiest food-lovers, fortunate to make a living writing about and researching food. Interviewing and engaging with chefs, industry professionals, and the most forward-thinking figures in the business as a food magazine editor has provided insight and endless inspiration. I am constantly surrounded by the greatest of friends and like-minded food-lovers, all responsible for

enriching my style, my appreciation, my knowledge—and my daily life.

Every job that I've ever held has been in the food business (with the exception of a very short-lived and horribly misguided stint at the Gap during one abysmal holiday season). By some divine providence, I also found myself at work in the craft beer business just as the public had begun to demand the same quality- and ingredient-driven ethos en vogue in the food scene from beverages as well.

Shortly after its founding, the Bruery in Orange County, California, hired me. During the years that followed, I received not only an education in all things beer (eventually becoming a Certified Cicerone—a position comparable to a sommelier in the wine world) but also in business and in flavor development.

Patrick Rue, the company's founder and owner, is to my mind one of the most gifted flavor developers in the food and beverage industries. His beers are at once classic and traditional yet off-the-wall creative. Working with Patrick, being privy to his thought processes, observing the growth of and consumer appreciation for his wildly successful brewery and totally original line of products (in an increasingly creative market), I learned to think about taste without the limitations of genre, cuisine, public expectation, or application.

The years spent with the company were the most formative in my food and writing career and also in the way that I came to understand flavor. Both with the Bruery and through becoming a Cicerone, I was simultaneously cataloging the principles of flavor development and pairing and watching those guidelines expertly exercised—not only at my brewery but also across the industry. It was an exhilarating time to be a part of the exploding American beer business and, by association, the food and restaurant world as well.

I was geek-ified me in the best way possible; it was a school of thought in which a strong understanding of the science behind the product was critical to its creation. I had always allowed whim to steer the ship when making something at home (often with less than desirable results). And the restaurants at which I'd waited tables or tended bar over the years were hardly in the habit of educating servers in culinary science.

Eventually, missing my family and friends on the flip side, I moved back to the Northeast. I met and married Emily, who adhered to a similar take-it-seriously spirit when it came to her personal craft (perhaps somewhat ironically, given that the skill in question was stand-up comedy). Together we traveled extensively and ate adventurously and often, and with each new experience, I became more inspired.

And while I had learned to love beer completely, my heart was still thoroughly fastened to the freezer section. I knew that I wanted to comprehend my craft in the way that my wife and my brewer friends commanded theirs.

I began reading like a maniac: consumer ice cream cookbooks, academic resources, journals from food science programs—ones geared toward professionals, researchers, or even massive conglomerates producing ice cream. I wanted the nitty-gritty, not just the recipes, so I went on to enroll in Penn State University's Ice Cream Short Course, a famed 120-year program that has played host to everyone from Ben & Jerry to Jeni Britton Bauer—ice cream icons across generations.

With a sturdy collegiate-level base of ice cream knowledge, years of personal experimentation, and the inspiration from Emily and my friends, family, and beer biz buddies, I finally felt confident that I could transform the things that I'd learned about life and love, about beer and dairy, into something I could share with the people around me.

For me, ice cream became a conduit through which to tell stories. To re-create and riff on memories, to spin recollections into something shareable, scoopable—

something that could inspire memories for others the way that it had always done for me.

It became a way to take what Rosie had initiated, what a decade and a half in the food industry had elaborated upon, and what my friends at the Bruery and in the writing community had helped solidify simply by being their creative, inquisitive, and authentic selves.

I'm sometimes told that I can be a little romantic when I write about food, and I won't deny it. It seems appropriate as a manifestation of my lifelong love. I've cared deeply for so many different foods over the years, had occasional but intense relationships with a range of ingredients and dishes—affairs with avocado, a fling with fava beans. But for me, ice cream has and always will be *the one*.

Consider this book my long-form love letter to the stuff.

# A MANIFESTO OF ICE CREAM MAGIC

If you're still not quite sold on the idea of *Yet Another Ice Cream Cookbook,* I can't say I blame you. In fact, I've *been* you.

I know from personal experience that the category of ice cream cookbooks can, at times, feel a bit homogenous, replete with refashioned compendiums, many composed of a familiar flavor kaleidoscope: the vanillas and chocolates, the butter pecans and mint chips, the hot fudge and the butterscotch. And look, there's nothing wrong with that. Those flavors practically raised me. But they've been done, and they've been done *really* well. Many of those books have informed the way that I make ice cream today.

Yet you've come as far as this page. Maybe because it's hot outside or because the cover image just beckoned. Maybe you're killing time while your shopping partner makes the rounds in the romance novel or sci-fi section. Or maybe—just maybe—you had hoped to find a departure from the dozens of other ice cream cookbooks you've come across.

So before you walk away in the direction of the mall's food court for a quick and dirty Ben & Jerry's fix, I ask that you at least leaf through these pages. I think you might just be pleasantly surprised!

See, I knew if I was going to get into the business, I'd have to make it my goal to share something compelling, something truly new. There were so many amazing ice cream makers already, ones that I myself admired so dearly. I didn't want to reproduce; I just loved ice cream too damn much to dilute the market with anything less than outstanding.

With that in mind, I decided that I'd never attempt to re-create flavors or offerings that were personal or cultural favorites. Inventiveness became most important to me—not out of irreverence but, rather, out of respect.

What has always been my priority is to forever remain ice cream's number one, crazy-face-painted, giant-foam-finger-in-the-air fan. I never wanted to be an ice cream maker to become tedious, for a lifetime of loving the stuff to suddenly be ruined by the banalities of repetition or by bottom-line-accommodating compromise.

Ultimately, my philosophy became informed by my obsession with turning everything I eat and everything that inspires me into an ice cream. And with turning ice cream into everything I eat. I've long been fascinated by what else ice cream can do. My love of it in every flavor, under any circumstance, and in any setting made me feel like there was more to it somehow. As if ice cream was begging me to just give it a chance to shine. Like some restless heir to the family business, it respected what generations of its ice cream ancestry had established, but it had something more to prove to the world. And yes, I *am* telling you that ice cream speaks to me.

I quickly realized just how many

parameters we've placed around the enjoyment of ice cream. It's got to be scooped. Eaten in a cup or a cone, usually in warm weather. Flavors should always be sweet, and don't dare touch the stuff before dinner—you'll spoil your appetite. We've put ice cream in a box, and that box is about 4 cubic feet and sits above our refrigerators.

I knew that ice cream would need to be liberated. It needed to be set free. *I* needed to be set free. So what would happen if Willy Wonka took up ice cream instead of chocolate making? Whatever the answer was, that's what I wanted my ice cream to be.

And because good ol' fashioned laziness is sometimes the mother of invention, you'll also notice that many of these recipes were created with simplicity in mind. I've included some variations that satisfy a frozen treat frenzy but can be executed quickly and with few ingredients—even some that can be made with the store-bought stuff of your choice.

Using high-quality components also helps simplify the process. If you let them, ideal ingredients will do most of the heavy lifting; firm and fresh cherries don't need a ton of processing to make perfect cherry ice cream.

There isn't a single recipe for chocolate ice cream because, thanks to high-quality dark chocolate that isn't diluted by dairy, I think you'll find one scoop of the sorbet in this book to be a far more decadent, hit-the-spot fix.

And I don't get hung up on technicalities. There's an entire section devoted to ice cream recipes that aren't actually ice creams at all but, rather, fast and easy twists on frozen desserts with so few ingredients, you won't even need a grocery list. They're not *technically* ice cream, but I believe they can lick any frozen dessert lusting—and even create a few new ones.

This book is all about enjoying the magic of ice cream. It's about tasting familiar flavors in a whole new way and allowing our imaginations to engineer freely and without boundaries or preconceived notions. And to combine some of the perks of being grown up—like drinking a great beer or being exposed to an amazing meal in a restaurant—to influence our ice cream experience now.

So let's think outside the box. In fact, let's throw the damn box out (or recycle it—whatever your municipality prefers) and let's start over. Let's unlearn what we've learned about ice cream and just let it be itself.

It's my hope that by the time you're through reading this book cover to cover (which you're totally going to do, right?), you'll have no problem creating classic flavors—or your own concoctions—with what you've learned.

Buying this book grants you entry into an exclusive frozen dessert faction, and together, we will begin our journey. I won't sugarcoat this for you: There will be challenges on the path to this ice cream enlightenment. I can commit only to my end of this bargain, as I attempt to indoctrinate you into the ice cream kingdom. But you'll need to enter with an open mind and an empty freezer.

# THE BUSINESS OF ICE CREAM BASICS

Before we dig into the scoops, we've got to talk a little bit about the science. I know what you're thinking—*bor-r-ring*. But hold it right there. Learning a little bit of chemistry through the colored lens of something so completely delicious can be super fun.

Besides, as Dakota Fanning once preached in the highly underrated 2003 film *Uptown Girls*, fundamentals are the building blocks of fun. I'll briefly review the CliffsNotes on what ice cream is and what wonderful ingredients will sacrifice their lives to make your dessert worth dying for.

But first, let's take it way back. What is this *ice cream*? At its most basic, ice cream is a foam. It's an emulsion that includes some combination of milk, cream, sugar, and other customizable items that serve different functions. These ingredients respectively contribute proteins, fats, air, water, and sugars, which, when frozen together under agitation, produce a creamy, cold product that remains soft enough to scoop even at subzero temperatures.

That magical ability is thanks to a phenomenon known as freezing point depression, courtesy of salts, sugars, and other solutes in the mixture. When these substances are dissolved in the right ratios, they prevent the mix from freezing solid. The air whipped in during agitation is what keeps it fluffy and creamy, and your imagination is what keeps it interesting.

Questions? Not yet? Splendid. Let's move on, shall we?

## IN THE MIX

What is ice cream "mix"?

In the biz, *mix* is a term used to describe the liquid created to eventually be frozen and transformed into the perfect product we know as ice cream.

Creating a balanced and well-formulated base mix is, to Ms. Fanning's point, the most critical of steps. The mix is calibrated to ensure that it can capture and retain that air that we work so hard to whip in during the spinning process.

Each ingredient in the mix needs to be carefully selected and calibrated in the proper ratios in order to achieve the most exquisitely enjoyable end product.

### DAIRY

Dairy selection and ratio are critical, and the amount of water that each brings to the mix is a pendulum with a vast swing. Heavy (or whipping) cream has a fat content of about 40%, whereas skim milk is nearly entirely $H_2O$.

Your dairy combination will determine the percentage of butterfat in your ice cream. Commercially, the FDA requires that ice cream has a minimum of 10% butterfat, which is why when you buy diet, low-fat, or low-calorie ice cream products, you'll often see them referred to as frozen desserts—

they're not legally ice cream! I've looked into this on their behalf, and while I don't think they're in any real danger of being arrested, they definitely can be cited for being a whole lot less delicious.

Fat is particularly important to at-home ice cream making because many don't want to use or don't have ready access to commercially employed emulsifier/stabilizer combos. Butterfat is naturally effective at pulling off the tasks assigned to those ingredients: Higher butterfat means more solids and less moisture in the mix and less need for emulsifying and stabilizing agents to wrangle water.

## NONFAT DRY MILK

The sweet cream or "blank" recipe in this book calls for nonfat dry milk, a powdered dairy product that has been relieved of all fat and water, leaving behind what are referred to as milk solids (delicious, eh?). These granules contain all the good stuff in milk—the proteins and sugars—without the moisture.

Nonfat dry milk helps improve the texture, providing a bit of chewiness and working in tandem with the butterfat in liquid dairy to contribute to structural integrity. When heated in the mix, this stuff also happens to create one of my favorite smells, the caramelization of the lactose causing a slightly "cooked" aroma that reminds me of the warm milk my mom served me as a soothing bedtime snack.

## STARCH

The omission of eggs in the recipe means that we're going without the natural stabilizer that comes standard in a custard base. Starch is an effective thickening agent that helps add body and bind that pesky liquid.

## SUGAR

When it comes to sugar, it's not all created, well, *equal*. The white stuff we had when we were kids—you know, the kind we used to eat straight out of the packet?—just doesn't have a place in this mix. It's highly refined, and its only real remaining flavor is *sweet*.

Unless otherwise noted, the recipes in this book all employ organic cane sugar, but you'll see a number of sweeteners throughout the subsequent pages.

**ORGANIC CANE SUGAR/DEMERARA:** This is the standard sugar in the recipes in this book. It's less refined than white sugar; it actually retains some of the natural color and flavor of real sugarcane juice and is fuller bodied and a bit caramel-like. It also manages to hold on to the nutrients that would have been stripped away by the time it became common table sugar.

**LIGHT MUSCOVADO:** It has a moister, finer grain than organic cane sugar. Old-school brown sugar is simply white sugar with molasses added back into the mix, while muscovado is produced from the natural retention of sugarcane juice.

**DARK MUSCOVADO:** Full of rich, sticky goodness, this is the boldest of the sugar set. It works beautifully in savory settings as well.

Though the use of less refined sugars may mean a slightly less milky-white base,

I think you'll find far more greatness grain for grain and that overall the recipes require *less* sugar to produce far more flavor.

Sugar is also critical to the freezing point and to what we call scoopability.

## SALT

Salt is nature's most critical ingredient in any dish. Adding a little bit of salt to something sweet elevates each bite. Unless otherwise specified, we're talking about kosher salt, although you'll also find a number of recipes that incorporate a flaky sea salt for texture.

When it comes to flakes, Maldon is a classic French product that is fairly widely available. There are also some fantastic stateside producers of the saline stuff. I love the Meadow and Jacobsen Salt Company. Each is harvesting and offering multiple variants and flavor-infused salts. These are a great way to add a little extra twist without needing to adjust the recipe dramatically or mess with the existing formula.

## CORN SYRUP

The court of public opinion has vacillated, largely on the offensive against this product, in recent years. However, when we talk about its use here, we're not referring to high fructose corn syrup but, rather, its less refined relative. Does that mean the stuff is a health food? Absolutely not. And I do not endorse drinking it, bathing in it, or dressing your salads with it. But ice cream is by nature an indulgence, meant to be enjoyed in moderation, and I try to keep the use of corn syrup to a bare minimum.

The ingredient is used because it inhibits crystallization—it helps keep your scoops creamy. This is important to at-home ice cream making because we are already starting out with a boulder at the bottom of a very large hill, and we need to find ways to compete with our commercial counterparts without the advantages of their equipment.

If you're super wary, I advocate reading the labels of corn syrup bottles before purchasing; some manufacturers sneak the high fructose variety into the standard version. There are also brands that include artificial vanilla flavoring, which will ultimately mess with your mix's flavor.

Can honey or agave nectar be used as a substitute? The answer, in short, is yes. Those sweeteners can have a similar effect; however, they come with distinctive flavors all their own.

## WHY IS AGING IMPORTANT?

These recipes recommend that your mix be "aged" overnight in the refrigerator. This extra, time-consuming step is sometimes a point of contention for the impatient (myself included). So what's the big idea? There is a whole bunch of geeky science involved, but in short, it gives the mix time to breathe, the ingredients a chance to get to know each other, and the chemistry we kept in mind when we calibrated the mix to come into play.

You still want that scientific stuff? It involves the partial coalescence of fat globules and the hydration of proteins. Translation? Aging makes ice cream *creamier*. The "overrun," the industry term for the air whipped into the ice cream, is also affected by the aging process, as it helps contribute to structural stability.

Of utmost importance should you decide to roll the dice and run the machine sans the aging is that the mix be *cold*. Pouring warm mix into an ice cream machine puts your poor spinner at an unfair disadvantage by forcing it to first cool down the mix and then freeze it. Freezer bowls in particular are not well suited to such tasks.

So, do you absolutely need to age your mix? I suggest you do. But if you just cannot wait and there are extenuating circumstances—like, POTUS just popped in and asked you to real quick make him some ice cream before his next meeting with world leaders—you'll at least want to make sure your mix is chilled below 40°F before you attempt to freeze it. Otherwise, it won't be of presidential quality.

## TOOLS

By default, ice cream making requires at least one piece of specialized, countertop-consuming equipment. As such, it's my mission to keep additional barriers to entry—like the need to buy up a bunch of gadgets and gizmos—to a minimum.

When it comes to choosing tools, I try to utilize those typically already hiding in most kitchens. You will find a flavor or two that requires a little something extra, but I'll always attempt to include an alternate method when possible.

If I had an ice cream–making superhero utility belt, however, these are the trusty implements that I'd have on my hip at all times.

### ICE CREAM MAKER

Just like when you buy a new car, you'll be confronted with models of all shapes and sizes. I believe I've tried almost all of them; naturally, there are pros and cons to each.

If we omit the over-$500 Aston Martin–esque set and the John Deere tractor–like hand-crank machines (which are fun for kids' birthday parties but more novel than efficient), we're left with two main categories: the freezer bowl and the continuously freezing.

The advantage to a continuously freezing machine is most evident in the planning stage. There's no need to worry about freezing your bowl at least 24 hours in advance because it has a built-in compressor. Simply plug it in and pour in your mix, and you'll have ice cream good to go without much additional foresight. It allows you to make multiple batches back to back; when using a freezer bowl machine, you'll need to remember to freeze an additional bowl should you want to churn more than one flavor.

This BMW-level luxury comes with a corresponding price tag for convenience, in this case starting around $300. If you're an avid experimenter, this might be the way to go, but if you feel like you're more of a fair-weather frozen dessert-maker, or you're just looking to cut your teeth on a more practical piece of equipment, the next category is your speed.

The freezer-bowl–based at-home machine is the most approachable for the novice, thanks to its price point (you can pick up one of these reliable and practical compact car–style machines for around $60). You can also buy backup bowls for about $25, but keep in mind that you'll need the additional freezer real estate.

While the slow spin speed and rapidly thawing bowl can present challenges, if you give your mix and your preparation the proper attention, you'll be able to execute creamy, creatively satisfying concoctions with this classic tool.

## IMMERSION BLENDER WITH FOOD PROCESSOR ATTACHMENT

This tool, perhaps even more so than the ice cream machine, is the most important one in my kitchen. If I were a Ninja Turtle (and in a frequently occurring daydream, I am), this would totally be my signature weapon. I'd strap it to my shell and whip it out whenever villainy was afoot, certain that my trusty stick blender would always save the day.

The version I recommend comes with a food processor attachment, meaning you can consolidate your kitchen tools (I am a fan of anything that can pull double duty). If you aren't able to get your hands on this amped-up optional package, the original still gets most of the jobs in this book done. It will be your best friend, helping you create each fresh batch of the creamiest product possible.

## STAND OR HAND MIXER

If you have a stand mixer, life is that much simpler. Freezer bowl attachments are available that preclude purchasing a separate ice cream maker altogether! If you're a regular at-home cook, purchasing one is worthwhile even if you never attempt a single ice cream, because of its versatility in making savory to sweet treats, breads to brownies, pastas to pastries.

If you haven't had a wedding or similar opportunity to *gently* nudge relatives into presenting you with one of these puppies, a basic hand mixer can execute as well.

## MICROPLANE

Citrus zest is one of my favorite ingredients. It is critical to something like the Grapefruit-Honey Softer-Serve recipe (page 105) but can also add dimension and depth to unsuspecting items like Mint Cherry Compote (page 26). A Microplane is also useful for grating spices and cheeses.

## CANDY THERMOMETER

I'm strongly opposed to cluttering up a kitchen with extraneous items, but I really do recommend having one of these on hand. While it isn't *entirely* indispensable—there are old-school ways to gauge the doneness of caramels or guesstimate the temperature of oil when frying doughnuts—it is infinitely less frustrating to purchase an $8 item than to toss an entire batch of something and start from scratch.

# CHAPTER 1

# PARTNERS IN CREAM

We all need a little help from our friends. This first section explores the accoutrements that play supporting roles in each sweet success. Some will find their way into the following ice creams as inclusions or variegates or into alternate creations in this book. Others simply stand alone, hoping to land starring roles of their own.

Once you've harnessed your own inspirations, you can use this section to mix and match, improvise, and improve upon recipes to make them your own. Each of these recipes is a building block, a foundation on which future frozen dreams are to be divined.

SEA-SALTED CHOCOLATE-
COVERED PECAN TOFFEE 18

CHOCOLATE SNAPS 20

MALTED SALTED TOFFEE 21

SPICY PUMPKIN SEED
CRUNCH 23

MAPLE-MOLASSES
CRANBERRY SAUCE 24

HONEYED PEANUT BUTTER
SAUCE 25

MINT CHERRY COMPOTE 26

GINGER HIBISCUS SYRUP 27

LEMON CURD 28

COFFEE CARAMEL SAUCE 30

HONEY MUSTARD SWIRL 31

TOMATO CARAMEL SAUCE 33

MEXICAN MUSCOVADO
CARAMEL SAUCE 34

MALTED HOT FUDGE 35

MARSHMALLOW WHIFF 36

BOURBON GANACHE 37

ENCHANTED SHELL 39

QUICK PICKLED BERRIES 40

MELTED ICE CREAM
GANACHE 42

SIMPLE STRAWBERRY JAM 43

## WHIPS

SEA-SALTED WHIP 45

PEYCHAUD'S BITTERS WHIP 45

HIBISCUS WHIP 47

IMPERIAL STOUT WHIP 47

# SEA-SALTED
# CHOCOLATE-COVERED
MAKES 6 CUPS *PECAN TOFFEE*

Don't make this stuff. Seriously. Don't do it.

And there. Now you can't say I didn't warn you. It is astounding how quickly the simple act of executing this recipe can deteriorate into a showdown with your own willpower. A quality-control sample turns into a quick snack. A handful invariably becomes a bucketful. There's just no way to resist something that has it all: It's crunchy, salty, sweet, chocolaty, and nutty.

I recommend a 75% dark chocolate, which is important to balance the significant sweetness natural to toffee. The acidity and slight bite from a high-quality chocolate provide the relief your palate needs to reset, and the crunchy salt elevates the entire affair.

### MEET ITS MATCH

Apart from drowning this stuff in ice cream or simply introducing palmfuls to your face, I also like to package it up and parcel it out during the holidays to well-deserving parties. My family has come to expect a tiny burlap sack loaded with toffee to be attached to their Christmas gifts—and in some cases, it just may preclude the need for a larger present altogether!

2 cups coarsely chopped pecans

1 cup unsalted butter

2 cups sugar

1 1/2 cups chopped 75% dark chocolate

Flaked sea salt (such as Maldon), for sprinkling

1   On a baking sheet lined with parchment paper, spread the pecans.

2   In a small saucepan over medium-high heat, cook the butter and sugar together until they register 300°F on a candy thermometer.

3   Working quickly (and carefully!), pour the hot sugar mixture over the pecans.

4   While the mixture is still hot, use an offset spatula to spread the chocolate evenly over it and allow the chocolate to melt. Sprinkle liberally with the flaked sea salt.

5   Allow to cool completely, then chop the toffee into bite-size pieces.

# CHOCOLATE SNAPS

Chocolate chips are classic, of course—perhaps even ice cream's oldest friend. But the store-bought cookie-destined kind aren't necessarily intended to swim in subzero situations. When standard chips are frozen in ice cream, they can become extremely hard and, thus, relatively flavorless. That's not to mention the danger they pose to dental work.

This preparation makes the chocolate pieces less like chips and more like a snap; hence the name. They're thin and ever so malleable, maintaining a bit of initial resistance but then evanescing when introduced to body temperature. Because they melt in your mouth, the chocolate flavor blooms on the palate in a big way, contrary to the effect of their tasteless, drop-shaped cousins.

### MEET ITS MATCH

**These are used specifically for Sage Chocolate Chip Ice Cream** *(page 58)* **and Roasted Cherry Chocolate Snap Ice Cream** *(page 86)*, **but they're a welcome addition to any recipe you might want to choco-fy.**

**4 ounces 70% or higher dark chocolate, finely chopped**

**1½ tablespoons canola oil (or coconut oil, but it will contribute a coconut flavor)**

1. Line a baking sheet with parchment paper.

2. In a double boiler over medium-high heat, combine the chocolate and oil. Stir regularly until the chocolate is melted. Pour over the parchment-lined baking sheet and spread evenly with a heatproof spatula.

3. Allow the mixture to cool completely and set. Once set, break into bite-size pieces and store in an airtight container until ready to use.

4. Refrigerate the snaps, as they will be more susceptible to melt at room temperature once tempered.

# MALTED SALTED *TOFFEE* MAKES 3 CUPS

Salty, malty, and wonderful. Originally developed for Bananas Ferrari Ice Cream (page 62), this is a versatile inclusion or topping that can add a little texture and depth to any inspired flavor.

½ cup butter

1 cup sugar

2 tablespoons water

2 tablespoons malted milk powder

1 teaspoon flaked sea salt

1  Line a baking sheet with parchment paper.

2  In a medium heavy-bottomed saucepan, combine the butter, sugar, water, and malted milk powder.

3  Cook over medium-high heat until the mixture registers 290°F on a candy thermometer. Working quickly, spread over the parchment-lined baking sheet. Sprinkle liberally with the flaked sea salt.

4  Allow to cool completely, then chop (or crack) the toffee into bite-size pieces. Store in an airtight container for up to 1 week.

## MEET ITS MATCH

Churn some chunks into your Chocolate Sorbet (page 65), or top your favorite butterscotch pudding recipe with this toffee for a crunchy counterpoint.

# SPICY
# PUMPKIN SEED CRUNCH

In this book, the brittle is broken up and used to spice up that saucy lady, Señorita Pepitas Ice Cream (page 89), but it's a sassy little snack on its own. It makes another great gift when wrapped up and packed in a pleasant little tin.

1 cup organic cane sugar

1 cup light muscovado sugar

2½ cups pumpkin seeds

8 tablespoons butter

½ teaspoon ground red pepper

½ teaspoon ground cinnamon

1 tablespoon chopped fresh rosemary

1 tablespoon sea salt, divided

## MEET ITS MATCH
Garnish a **Pumpkin Pie Shake** *(page 189)*, or bring a bag to munch on during your favorite fall football matchup.

1  Line a baking sheet with parchment paper. In a small saucepan over medium heat, melt the sugars until amber colored. Add the pumpkin seeds and butter and cook for 2 to 4 minutes, or until the seeds are toasted. Stir in the pepper, cinnamon, rosemary, and half of the salt.

2  Cook until the mixture registers 280°F on a candy thermometer. Using an offset spatula, spread over the baking sheet. Sprinkle with the remaining salt.

3  Allow to cool completely, then chop the brittle into bite-size pieces.

# MAPLE-MOLASSES
MAKES 1¾ CUPS *CRANBERRY SAUCE*

This Bog Cabin (page 92) variegate was developed to highlight New England's finest exports.

### MEET ITS MATCH
Use as a topping for Melted Ice Cream Pancakes *(page 134)*, swirl into Oatmeal Cinnamon Ice Cream *(page 97)*, or add a dollop to The Only Oatmeal You'll Ever Need *(page 133)* for a killer breakfast. Swap it for your standard canned cran at the Thanksgiving table for a festive take on the turkey.

1 cup maple syrup

1 cup molasses

1 cup fresh cranberries

¼ cup water

1  In a medium saucepan, cook the maple syrup, molasses, cranberries, and water, stirring regularly, until well integrated and the cranberries begin to pop and break.

2  Allow to cool completely, and then, using an immersion blender, puree until the cranberries are integrated and the mixture is smooth.

# HONEYED
MAKES 2½ CUPS
# PEANUT BUTTER SAUCE

There is hardly anything more American than a deep and unyielding love of peanut butter. We pledge allegiance to the snack that has rivers of the stuff, preferably supported by its rotating and loyal entourage—one that includes similarly bright stars of the silver spoon like chocolate, strawberry or grape jelly, and caramel. Honey has long pined for peanut butter's affection, too, but has had less luck winning its attention.

So when attempting to emulate some of the sundae toppings of standard ice cream parlors, I swapped out the commonly used dosage of corn syrup, rekindling an old friendship between peanut butter and this far more well-suited liquid sweetener.

1 cup smooth peanut butter
1 cup honey
½ cup heavy cream

1 In a small saucepan over low heat, gently warm the peanut butter, honey, and cream, stirring frequently, until smooth and well integrated.

2 Allow to cool completely and store in an airtight container.

## MEET ITS MATCH
Spread on toast with Quick Pickled Berries *(page 40)* for a twisted PB&J. Drizzle over Vanilla, Olive Oil & Cacao Nib Softer-Serve *(page 116)*.

# MINT CHERRY *COMPOTE* MAKES 1 CUP

This chewy, jammy condiment can be paired with savory or sweet dishes. Don't love mint and cherries? Try cranberries and sage. Or raisins and basil.

- ¼ cup organic cane sugar
- ⅔ cup dried cherries
- ⅔ cup water
- 20 leaves fresh mint

1   In a small saucepan over medium heat, cook the sugar, cherries, water, and mint for about 5 minutes, or until the cherries soften and reconstitute.

2   Remove from the heat and puree it in a food processor. Allow to cool completely and store in an airtight container.

### MEET ITS MATCH

**Serve as an accoutrement for a cheese plate, layer into a yogurt parfait with granola, or stir into mashed potatoes for an impressive dinner party introduction.**

**ROCKY ROAD TRIP**

## SOUTHERN CALIFORNIA

### ▼ GELATERIA ULI

In the historic Spring Arcade Building in downtown Los Angeles, Gelateria Uli is creating some of the best genuinely hand-crafted gelato in the country with the sharpness and attention to scientific detail that can only be explained by owner Uli Nasibova's background in the finance world.

Often inspired by impeccable California produce, flavors rotate regularly, and on any given day you can spot Uli herself hard at work through the picture window that provides a glimpse into her workspace. Give her a wave before grabbing yourself an affogato and enjoying her meticulous and deftly designed signatures.

**WHAT I'M HAVING:** The Horchata Gelato is an absolute killer, so two sizeable scoops, plus whatever inventive sorbet Uli has come up with for the season.

# GINGER HIBISCUS

MAKES 2 CUPS *SYRUP*

Hibiscus is such a startlingly, delicious flavor that's tart and sweet. The spicy ginger lends balance, and this syrup brings a little Zen to every application.

3 cups water

1 cup dried hibiscus flowers

3/4 cup light muscovado sugar

3/4 cup organic cane sugar

Zest of 1 lemon

1 vanilla bean (both the scraped seeds and the pod)

1/2"–1" piece fresh ginger, peeled and smashed (more if you're feeling extra spicy)

## MEET ITS MATCH
Use in cocktails or milkshakes or add 2 tablespoons to 1 cup of seltzer water for homemade Ginger Hibiscus Soda.

1 In a medium saucepan over medium heat, combine the water, flowers, sugars, lemon zest, vanilla bean, and ginger.

2 Bring to a boil, and then reduce the heat to a simmer. Cook for 30 to 40 minutes, or until the mixture is reduced by about three-quarters.

3 Remove from the heat. Using cheesecloth or a fine-mesh strainer, remove the solids.

4 Allow the syrup to cool completely and store in an airtight container.

# LEMON *CURD*  MAKES ¾ CUP

This stuff makes me severely wish I hadn't avoided eating the stuff my whole life simply because of its name. The custardy, creamy, and bright flavor of lemon curd is something I constantly crave—breakfast, lunch, dinner and dessert.

3 egg yolks

½ cup organic cane sugar

¼ cup lemon juice

Zest of 1 lemon

4 tablespoons butter, cubed

### MEET ITS MATCH

Layer into Better-Than-Buttermilk Biscuits *(page 132)*, spread on bagels or toast, use it as a filling for pastries and cakes, or toss with roasted Brussels sprouts, pistachios, and fresh linguini. Or simply enjoy it on its own in a bowl, with a spoon, stippled with fresh blueberries and basil.

1 Fill a small saucepan with about an inch of water. Bring to a boil over high heat, then reduce to a simmer.

2 In a small bowl, whisk the egg yolks and sugar until smooth. (Reserve the egg whites and make Pavlova!) Add the lemon juice and lemon zest and continue to whisk.

3 Set the bowl over the simmering water, being careful that it does not touch the water. Continue to whisk regularly for 8 to 10 minutes, or until the curd has thickened to the consistency of a pudding.

4 Remove from the heat and, working in batches, stir in the butter until completely melted and well integrated.

5 Allow to cool completely and store in an airtight container in the refrigerator.

# COFFEE CARAMEL
**MAKES 1½ CUPS** *SAUCE*

The world really loves its caramel macchiatos. And while I prefer the more traditional espresso-centric drink with just a dollop of steamed milk, it's undeniable that there is still a time and place for our caffeinated cravings to make caramel's acquaintance.

1 cup organic cane sugar

1 cup dark muscovado sugar

1 cup brewed coffee

2 vanilla beans

1 teaspoon flaked sea salt

### MEET ITS MATCH
**Drizzle over cakes or cupcakes, swirl into Oatmeal Cinnamon Ice Cream** (page 97) **or Chocolate Sorbet** (page 65), **or whip into buttercream frosting. Or combine with ½ teaspoon of ground red pepper and spoon over aggressively seared and salted steaks.**

1  Prepare an ice bath in which to transfer your finished product by filling a large glass bowl with ice.

2  In a medium, light-colored saucepan (this will allow you to keep a good eye on the changing color of the caramel) over medium heat, combine the sugars and coffee.

3  Cook for 5 to 7 minutes, or until the sugars are dissolved and the mixture is smooth. Be sure the sugars are completely dissolved before the mixture comes to a boil. This will ensure that the caramel is creamy and avoids becoming gritty.

4  Continue to cook until the mixture is smoking slightly and quite dark. Remove from the heat and carefully stir in the vanilla beans and salt.

5  Shock the caramel by pouring it into a storage vessel set over your ice bath to stop the cooking. (I typically use a glass Pyrex-type bowl with a cover.) Allow the sauce to cool completely and store in an airtight container.

# HONEY MUSTARD

MAKES ¾ CUP

## SWIRL

This recipe is not terribly far from a traditional honey mustard, so standard uses apply. But once you've had a chance to get comfortable with the one-two punch of a sweet hook and a spice-spiked jab, I encourage playing with some other combinations. Find a bridge for the flavors; for example, cherries love both mustard and honey. As do smoky almonds or brown sugar or molasses. In fact, that's one big, happy, honey mustard family right there. See? Building another flavor around this stuff isn't sounding so crazy after all.

¾ cup honey

½ cup Dijon mustard

2 tablespoons melted butter

In a small bowl, whisk together the honey, mustard, and butter until smooth. Store in an airtight container in the refrigerator until ready to use.

## MEET ITS MATCH

Use as a dip for crudités or an alternate tangy dressing for a slaw. Or swirl into Brown Sugar Sour Cream Softer-Serve (page 108) with almonds and roasted cherries.

# TOMATO CARAMEL
MAKES ⅔ CUP *SAUCE*

**F**orget ketchup. This is the role tomato was born to play.

½ cup muscovado sugar
½ cup organic cane sugar
¾ cup water
½ cup tomato paste
1 teaspoon salt

1 Prepare an ice bath in which to transfer your finished product by filling a large glass bowl with ice.

2 In a medium saucepan over medium heat, combine the sugars and water. Slowly bring to a boil. Be sure to dissolve the sugar completely before the mixture comes to a boil. This will ensure that the caramel is creamy and avoids becoming gritty.

3 Cook until the mixture reaches 250°F on a candy thermometer and is copper colored.

4 Remove from the heat and carefully stir in the tomato paste and salt. The mixture will bubble violently. Allow the sauce to settle and stir until smooth. Return to the heat and cook until the mixture reaches 218°F.

5 Remove from the heat and shock the caramel by pouring it into a storage vessel set over your prepared ice bath to stop the cooking. (I typically use a glass Pyrex-type bowl with a cover.) Allow the sauce to cool completely and store in an airtight container.

### MEET ITS MATCH
**Combine with a tangy barbecue sauce, toss with grilled onions and place on a burger, drizzle over a goat's milk cheesecake, or garnish a decadently rich chocolate cake.**

# MEXICAN MUSCOVADO

MAKES 1¼ CUPS *CARAMEL SAUCE*

Somewhere along the way, we've become obsessed with salted caramel. Though salt has always been the Hillary to sugar's Bill, only recently have we begun recognizing its significance off the savory menu.

But I think in all our salt-centric confectionary scheming, we've done an injustice to another indispensable caramel ingredient: vanilla. Called for in extract form, practically as an afterthought, it's usually at the tail end when tallying ingredients, little consideration given to variety, contribution, or value. When you've gone so far as to select raw sugars or some pink Himalayan specialty sea salt, it's a disservice to the finished dish to fish out an ages-old bottle of extract at the very last minute.

To my mind, vanilla beans are one of the world's most flavorful, most impactful, and most criminally underestimated ingredients. This caramel was designed to highlight a single variety, but if it were up to me (and sometimes it is), all caramels would feature a vanilla bean or blend complementary to the final use. And while salt is certainly a caramel costar, I think it's time it shared the spotlight with an ingredient of equal gravity.

## MEET ITS MATCH

Accepted everywhere you want caramel to be.

2 Mexican vanilla beans
1 cup organic cane sugar
1 cup dark muscovado sugar
1 cup water
1 teaspoon flaked sea salt

1  Scrape the seeds from the vanilla bean pods and set aside. Reserve the pods for another use (like infusing your favorite rum or bourbon or simmering with a jam).

2  Prepare an ice bath in which to transfer your finished product by filling a large glass bowl with ice.

3  Over medium heat, in a light-colored saucepan (this will allow you to keep a good eye on the changing color of the caramel), combine the sugars and water.

4  Cook until the sugars are dissolved before the mixture comes to a boil, ensuring that the caramel is creamy and not gritty.

5  Continue to cook until the mixture is smoking slightly and quite dark. Remove from the heat and carefully stir in the salt and reserved vanilla bean seeds.

6  Shock the caramel by pouring it into a storage vessel set over your prepared ice bath to stop the cooking. (I typically use a glass Pyrex-type bowl with a cover.) Allow the sauce to cool completely and store in an airtight container.

# MALTED HOT FUDGE

MAKES 1⅙ CUPS

As the topic that's basically synonymous with the ice cream sundae, hot fudge has been reinterpreted, reinvented, and reimagined in hundreds of ways.

This is simply my humble contribution to the hot fudge anthology. When developing what I'd intended to be a signature fudge sauce, the concept of a malted chocolate shake kept coming to mind. A touch of molasses deepens the flavor and provides the bite necessary to balance the sweet malt.

This is a seriously sticky sauce that needs to be served warm in order to stay creamy and pourable. If you store your sauce for later use, it's best to do so in a glass jar that can be warmed in a water bath or in a microwaveable container; it'll be tricky to extract once cooled, and you'll need to reheat in order to serve.

⅔ cup heavy cream
¼ cup organic cane sugar
¼ cup unsweetened cocoa powder
1 tablespoon molasses
¼ cup corn syrup
½ teaspoon salt
½ cup malt powder
1 vanilla bean
½ cup finely chopped unsweetened chocolate

1 In a small saucepan over medium heat, whisk together the cream, sugar, cocoa, molasses, corn syrup, salt, and malt powder until well integrated.

2 Stir in the vanilla bean and chocolate and warm until the chocolate is melted and the mixture is smooth.

3 Remove the vanilla bean and store the topping in an airtight container in the refrigerator. Reheat when ready to use and serve warm.

### MEET ITS MATCH

Use as an all-purpose ice cream topping, a cake filling, or the basis for a thick and chewy milkshake, or spread over crusty toast with flaked sea salt as a snack. Go all-American by combining it with Honeyed Peanut Butter Sauce (page 25) and Sea-Salted Whip (page 45).

# MARSHMALLOW WHIFF

A riff on the classic marshmallow topping, this stuff is exceptional when torched, the bitter char offsetting some of its inherent sweetness. But if you'd rather not risk your ice cream's life by playing with fire, it's a versatile topping in its safer state as well.

1 egg white

¾ cup corn syrup

1 teaspoon salt

1 cup confectioners' sugar

1 teaspoon vanilla extract

1   In the bowl of a stand mixer, beat the egg white, corn syrup, and salt for 5 minutes, or until fluffy and doubled in volume. Reduce the mixer speed to low and add the sugar in batches, beating until well integrated. Add the vanilla and beat until just blended.

2   Store in an airtight container and refrigerate for up to 2 weeks.

## MEET ITS MATCH

It's great blowtorched on almost any ice cream, as a topping for ice cream cakes or a filling for cookie sandwiches, or sandwiched between crusty bread with Honeyed Peanut Butter Sauce (page 25).

---

**ROCKY ROAD TRIP**

## NEW YORK & CONNECTICUT

⊤ STEW LEONARD'S, MULTIPLE LOCATIONS

It's technically a grocery store, but those who have been fortunate enough to become acquainted with its ethos and eccentricities know that Stew Leonard's is a grocery store with *character*. And by "character," I mean singing cows and banjo-playing milk cartons—actual shopping-aisle-dwelling animatronics performing in concert, extolling the advantages of farm-fresh dairy or the virtues of fruits and vegetables.

Most important, thanks to Stew's dairy farm descent, a frozen treat stand bids you farewell as you exit the store; soft-serve ice creams and frozen yogurts with a selection of dips and toppings keep the kids occupied and perhaps make the parents (and big kids like yours truly) even happier.

The freshness of the dairy is indisputable, and the cones are among the creamiest in the country. And if you spend $100 on groceries, you're entitled to a free cone. Now that's my kind of customer loyalty program.

**WHAT I'M HAVING:** Vanilla & Chocolate Swirl with Rainbow Sprinkles—straight up

# BOURBON GANACHE

Sit down, chocolate—you're drunk.

**½ cup very finely chopped chocolate (see note)**

**¾ cup heavy cream**

**1½ tablespoons bourbon (or rye, scotch, or other spirit of your choice)**

1 Place the chocolate in a heatproof bowl and set aside.

2 In a small saucepan over medium heat, warm the cream until simmering. While hot, pour the cream over the reserved chocolate. Add the bourbon. Stir until the chocolate is melted and the mixture is creamy.

**NOTE:** This recipe is for a soft, pourable ganache that can be used as a ripple in ice cream or a topping. For a thicker ganache that can be used as a filling, increase the chocolate to 1 cup.

## SUGGESTED RIFF

**BOURBON GANACHE TRUFFLES:** Increase the chocolate to 1 cup and decrease the cream to ½ cup. Refrigerate the ganache for several hours. Using a melon baller or cookie dropper, scoop the ganache into balls, roll them in cocoa powder, and serve.

### MEET ITS MATCH
Dip strawberries into it, or serve it alone with a spoon as a pairing for a good cigar and a fireside chat.

# ENCHANTED SHELL

MAKES 1 CUP

The recipe for this, er, "enchanted" shell is reminiscent of the classic awe-inspiring first-it's-a-sauce-then-it's-a-solid, blink-and-you'll-miss-it ice cream topping. It's also the stuff into which Dairy Queen and Mister Softee cones dive headfirst before being upended and handed over. Where once was a fudgy-looking liquid is—*voilà!*—a firm and snappy shell. I still think it's a pretty damn cool party trick.

The secret ingredient is coconut oil, and while you can subtly taste its essence, you can further enhance your flavors by adding in a few drops of a complementary essential oil or an extract like peppermint, orange, almond, or vanilla.

As the shell will need to be reheated in order to magically transform, store these in a glass jar that can later be warmed in a water bath or in a microwaveable container.

### MEET ITS MATCH

**Perfect for Pint Bottom Bonbons** (page 142) **but adds an element of fun and flavor** to almost any ice cream. Use it to line a cone for a crunchy, chocolate-coconut finale.

## WHITE CHOCOLATE ENCHANTED SHELL

**2 cups finely chopped white chocolate**

**1/4 cup coconut oil**

1. Prepare a double boiler.

2. Over medium heat, combine the chocolate and oil and stir for 3 to 5 minutes, or until smooth and creamy.

3. Remove from the heat, allow to cool slightly, and then spoon over your ice cream of choice. The shell should harden within 20 to 30 seconds.

## DARK CHOCOLATE ENCHANTED SHELL

**2 cups finely chopped 72% dark chocolate**

**1/4 cup coconut oil**

1. Prepare a double boiler.

2. Over medium heat, combine the chocolate and oil and stir for 3 to 5 minutes, or until smooth and creamy.

3. Remove from the heat, allow to cool slightly, and then spoon over your ice cream of choice. The shell should harden within 20 to 30 seconds.

# QUICK PICKLED
MAKES ⅓ TO ½ CUP *BERRIES*

The beauty of these babies is that not only does the berry selection bring fresh, bright flavors to the table, but the pickling provides an acidic punch that cuts through the richness of many ice cream dishes.

As far as which berries to use, most work well, and the recipe is adaptable to the seasons—strawberries in summer, cranberries in fall. You can even pickle grapes or melon balls with this recipe. The spice profile is also entirely customizable.

### MEET ITS MATCH

**Use as a delicious topping for grilled meats, sandwiches, or hot dogs. Or try it mixed into soft and chewy caramels just before they set or as a counterpoint to creamy, mouth-coating cheeses.**

1 cup berries (cranberries, blueberries, and blackberries all work well)

¼ cup organic cane sugar

½ cup apple cider vinegar

1 tablespoon honey

1 stick cinnamon

½ teaspoon whole cloves

½ teaspoon salt

1 Place the berries in a heatproof bowl and set aside.

2 In a medium saucepan over medium heat, bring the sugar, vinegar, honey, cinnamon stick, cloves, and salt to a boil. Cook for 3 to 5 minutes, or until the sugar is completely dissolved. Remove the cinnamon stick and cloves. Allow the brine to cool slightly, then pour it over the reserved berries.

3 Allow to cool completely. Store in an airtight container in the refrigerator for up to 3 months.

# MELTED ICE CREAM GANACHE

MAKES 1¼ CUPS

Using a melted ice cream provides an opportunity to play with the flavor profile of the sauce while maintaining a luxuriously lush consistency.

### MEET ITS MATCH

Crossbreed desserts are all the rage (croissant-doughnut, anyone?), so make ice cream ganache cupcakes. I won't even take the credit (until you try to trademark them, of course).

½ cup finely chopped bittersweet or semisweet chocolate

1 cup melted ice cream—flavor of your choice! (caramel, peanut butter, and coffee are all personal favorites)

1 Place the chocolate in a heatproof bowl and set aside.

2 Cook the melted ice cream in a small saucepan over medium heat for 3 to 5 minutes, or until simmering. While hot, pour over the reserved chocolate and stir until the chocolate is melted and the mixture is creamy.

# SIMPLE STRAWBERRY

MAKES 1½ CUPS *JAM*

So simple, it practically makes itself. So customizable, it will be welcome in almost any setting. Add herbs, spices, or alternate sugars to achieve a variety of flavor profiles.

### MEET ITS MATCH

**Add tarragon and black pepper when pureeing, then serve over Ginger Lemonade Softer-Serve** (*page 106*) **with a drizzle of balsamic reduction. Fill your favorite pastries, spread on toast, or stir into bubbly for a strawberry Bellini.**

**1 pint strawberries, hulled**
**1 tablespoon organic cane sugar**
**1 tablespoon brown sugar**

1   Place the strawberries in a bowl. Toss with the sugars and allow to stand for 30 minutes, stirring occasionally, or until the strawberries have released their juices.

2   Pulse in a food processor until smooth. Store in an airtight container in the refrigerator.

# WHIPS

WHIPPED CREAM VARIATIONS are a fun way to
introduce a complementary flavor without having to commit to an
additional ice cream. They're highly customizable, so feel free to
swap flavors or change things up a bit without being too
concerned about ruining a recipe. Use the ratios as a guiding
formula; the cream is fairly forgiving.

# SEA-SALTED *WHIP*

It's the whipped cream you never knew you always wanted. The small bit of salt offsets the sweetness of so many desserts, making every one of them totally magical.

## MEET ITS MATCH
**Serve on everything. With a spoon.**

1 cup cold heavy cream

3 tablespoons organic cane sugar

¾ teaspoon sea salt

1 In the bowl of a stand mixer, combine the cream, sugar, and salt. Using the whisk attachment, beat the cream for 2 to 4 minutes, or until stiff peaks form. Serve immediately.

2 You can accelerate the process by chilling your bowl ahead of time.

# PEYCHAUD'S BITTERS

MAKES 2 CUPS *WHIP*

Peychaud's is pretty in pink and has a versatile flavor with licorice and floral notes, but this recipe can accommodate any flavor of bitters.

## MEET ITS MATCH
**Top off a scoop of PBBG Ice Cream** (page 73), **Mint Cherry Mascarpone Ice Cream** (page 84), **or *Cacio e Pepe Ice Cream*** (page 83).

1 cup heavy cream

2 tablespoons organic cane sugar

10 dashes of Peychaud's or other bitters

1 In the bowl of a stand mixer, combine the cream, sugar, and bitters. Using the whisk attachment, beat the cream for 2 to 4 minutes, or until stiff peaks form. Serve immediately.

2 You can accelerate the process by chilling your bowl ahead of time.

# HIBISCUS WHIP

A dollop with peanut butter on crostini makes a fun grown-up sandwich substitute.

**MEET ITS MATCH**
Spoon over Ginger Lemonade Softer-Serve *(page 106)*, **Chocolate Sorbet** *(page 65)*, **Key Lime Vanilla Bean Softer-Serve** *(page 108)*, or **Honeyed Peanut Butter Sauce** *(page 25)* with **Bourbon Ganache** *(page 37)*.

1 cup heavy cream

2 tablespoons organic cane sugar

3 tablespoons Ginger-Hibiscus Syrup
(page 27)

1 In the bowl of a stand mixer, combine the cream, sugar, and hibiscus syrup. Using the whisk attachment, beat the cream for 2 to 4 minutes, or until stiff peaks form. Serve immediately.

2 You can accelerate the process by chilling your bowl ahead of time.

# IMPERIAL STOUT WHIP

Imperial stouts, by definition, are rich and complex, typically with notes of coffee, chocolate, roasted malts, and dark or dried fruits. In this whip, those flavors are encouraged to bloom. Using it is like adding a little cream to your coffee.

**MEET ITS MATCH**
Try it with **Roasted Cherry Chocolate Snap Ice Cream** *(page 86)*, **Doughnut Ya Love Coffee Ice Cream (aka The Fuzz)** *(page 94)*, as the topping on a blue cheesecake, or over a scoop of **Salty Buttered Honey Ice Cream** *(page 80)* with **Quick Pickled Berries** *(page 40)*.

2 cups heavy cream

1/2 cup confectioners' sugar

2 tablespoons imperial stout

1 In the bowl of a stand mixer, combine the cream, sugar, and stout. Using the whisk attachment, beat the cream for 2 to 4 minutes, or until stiff peaks form. Serve immediately.

2 You can accelerate the process by chilling your bowl ahead of time.

# TASTING ICE CREAM

When I was studying to become a Certified Cicerone, there was a lot of emphasis on tasting beer. After existing within that world for so long, I found myself involuntarily "tasting" everything. I swirled and sniffed seltzer water, I measured the clarity of lemonade, and I searched for bitterness across a breadth of foods in which I'd previously never considered the need for bite. It became a subconscious tic.

Like anyone crazy about her craft, I believe that ice cream does deserve some of that deference as well. Most times I try to simply enjoy, but should you decide to properly size up your scoops, here are a few points to evaluate when emulating an expert ice cream taster.

## CONDITIONS

Just as when you are tasting beer or wine, it's important to create a proper tasting environment. Only in bright and neutral lighting will you have an accurate idea of color. The atmosphere should be free of interfering aromas like smoke or perfume. Your palate should be fresh, which means no smoking or coffee drinking prior to sampling.

## APPEARANCE

Obviously the first indicator of taste; your brain immediately begins to involuntarily evaluate food based on sight and the information you've already given it. If it's expecting dark chocolate ice cream and what's in your dish is a pale beige, that indicates that the reality may not be in accordance with your expectation.

Visual composition may also hint at the quality of ingredients, technique, and potential flaws. (Does it appear crumbly or dry? Greasy or clean? Are ice crystals visible?)

## AROMA

During my educational experience at Penn State's Ice Cream Short Course, a unique fact was pointed out to us: Ice cream is one of few foods—if not the only food—that has no real aroma. I see the wheels turning in your head. But, if you think about it, the smell that most folks associate with ice cream isn't ice cream at all—it's typically waffle cones, hot fudge, or another ice cream accompaniment.

Of course, ice cream does have an aroma, as do milk and cream and chocolate and vanilla and all of the wonderful things that we so meticulously select. The culminating smell, however, just happens to be suspended upon delivery.

When it comes to evaluation, this criterion requires some patience. With beer and wine, aromatic compounds are volatile, subject to speedy dissipation. The drinker must swiftly analyze the smell upon pouring (swirling is then a second-rate attempt to revitalize that smell). Ice cream demands the opposite. The aroma of ice

cream comes only as it begins to warm up, or "bloom."

Since supposedly 80% of taste is smell, this is a critical issue in eating ice cream and why the serving temperature is of such great importance. Ice cream aromas are typically experienced retro-olfactorily, meaning we observe the smell backward through our noses as we exhale after ingesting a bite. In our mouths is where our product animates, aromas volatilizing, flavors blooming, and melting behavior activating in the presence of body heat.

## MOUTHFEEL

Mouthfeel is a rather unappetizing word that relates to the body of a product. It is the evaluation step associated with our sense of touch.

A number of additional flaws can be detected at this stage, most obviously related to whether the ice cream is, in fact, creamy. Is it thick and chewy? Thin and watery? Does it coat your palate or slip off your tongue? Is there a crumbly or dry feeling? Is there a grittiness related to large ice crystals?

## TASTE

The part that we're most accustomed to observing may also be the biggest challenge to assess. Most of the time, we separate this into two categories: good and bad. With a more in-depth appraisal, larger questions are posed. Is there something off about the flavor? The dairy itself? Does it taste cooked or sour? Artificial? Eggy?

As with aroma, temperature impacts taste. Think back to your last brain freeze—it's not just mind-numbing; cold can interfere with our palate's ability to perceive flavor as well.

## MELTDOWN

Meltdown is another observable factor in ice cream. Low-fat or low-calorie "ice cream" often melts very quickly, and the liquid that remains tends to separate or be watery in appearance. Products that are higher in butterfat or have more milk solids maintain their shape and constitution better. Custards and egg-based ice creams have more staying power and maintain a substantial mouthfeel even during meltdown.

## TOOLS

Serious professional ice cream evaluators never use spoons. Believe it or not, spoons are actually unnecessary when eating ice cream. Because it is a semisolid product, there is no risk of it slipping away.

If you're going to use one, it should enter your mouth upside down, ice cream side first. The old-fashioned soup-spoon method introduces your tongue to metal first, which is believed to interfere with the way your palate interprets ice cream when it finally meets the frozen product.

## TEMPERATURE AND STORAGE

For the third time in two pages, I'll repeat myself: Temperature is critical to the enjoyment of ice cream. And here's yet another reason why.

The typical dipping cabinet for hard-scoop American-style ice cream clocks in somewhere between 0° and 6°F. Gelato, which is denser and has a less substantial fat content, can be served up to 12°F. Custard, or egg-based formulas, are looking at 10° to 20°F, while soft-serve can reach almost 25°F at the time of tasting.

Home freezers hover around 0°F, which is why your ice cream is vexingly rigid when you first retrieve it. If you attempt to eat it at this point, you'll not only wind up with some sad and possibly permanently maimed spoons but also, should you succeed in freeing up a few bites, your palate will seize up in self-preservation. It's simply too cold to taste.

This is a conversation familiar in the craft beer business. Commercial brands touting a "frost-brewed" process or similarly nonsensical claims (there simply is no such thing) are contributing to consumer confusion. Beer that shares a temperature with the surface of the moon at midnight has one singular flavor: *cold*.

Regardless of its comfortable resting temperature, any change to ambient climate will seriously upset your ice cream, throwing it into a tantrum referred to as thermal shock. This phenomenon takes place when ice cream is encouraged to melt slightly and then refreeze, resulting in enlarged ice crystals. The practice of removing a package from the freezer and allowing it to sit long enough to become scoopable, then returning it to the freezer, is a common cause.

Instead, use smaller containers that might hold single servings. This will also ensure that during packaging, your ice cream freezes faster and thus more efficiently, making for a creamier product.

Stanpac is an example of an ice cream packaging company that sells (both to businesses and consumers) 3- or 4-ounce ice cream cups that are not only ideally sized but also super fun and nostalgic.

When creating flavors with variegates or inclusions, you may have to do your layering in a larger bowl or container and then transfer portions into these cups, but it will be worth the extra step for the smooth and supple resulting scoop.

# CHAPTER 2

# ICE CREAM ROAD MAP

Who needs Rand McNally when you can have Rocky Road ahead? These recipes are meant to demonstrate some alternate routes to delicious territory when you've grown tired of traditional ice cream traffic. So try some of my favorites to get the lay of the land, and then consult your own internal ice cream compass to point the way to perfectly personal dessert destinations.

# BLANK ICE CREAM BASE

**MAKES ABOUT 1 QUART**

For the purposes of this book, this is the mother recipe, the mix upon which most formulas going forward will be based. We're going to gussy it up, dress it down, build it up, and totally dismantle it. Master this base and you will have not only a delicious and completely satisfying sweet cream ice cream all on its own but also a road map to follow in pursuing your own creative ice cream adventures.

This is also a relatively low-sugar base. When using high-quality, extremely fresh cream and milk, the dairy is beautifully rich and fragrant, often with notes of grass and a sweetness all its own. I couldn't sleep at night knowing the injustice I may have done to those generous cows if I'd negated all their hard work beneath a mountain of white sugar!

Thanks to its low sweetness level and the absence of eggs, this base allows anything we add to the ice cream to really pop when it tops your cone.

> 5 teaspoons cornstarch
> 1¾ cups whole milk, divided
> 1¾ cups heavy cream
> ½ cup organic cane sugar
> 5 tablespoons nonfat dry milk
> ½ teaspoon salt

1  In a small bowl, combine the starch with 3 tablespoons of the whole milk and whisk until smooth. Set aside.

2  In a nonreactive saucepan, combine the cream, sugar, nonfat dry milk, salt, and the remaining whole milk. Nonfat dry milk can be quite sticky when wet, so it will naturally clump. Whisk assertively to ensure that the dry ingredients are well incorporated and no lumps remain.

3  Set the pan over medium heat and whisk frequently. In the meantime, prepare an ice bath in which to transfer your finished product by filling a large glass bowl with ice.

4  Cook the base until it reaches a boil, then reduce the heat and simmer for 4 to 5 minutes. A longer simmer will produce more of a "cooked" flavor in the finished product. Extreme cooked character can be referenced as a defect in ice creams, but I find that a little bit of a longer cook caramelizes the sugars inherent to the dairy and brings out a bit of that natural, grassy sweetness.

5  Add the reserved starch-and-milk mixture and cook for 1 minute, stirring constantly with a rubber spatula. Remove from the heat and pour into a storage vessel set over the ice bath. (I typically use a glass Pyrex-type bowl with a cover, as the base will need to be stored after cooking.)

**6** Using an immersion blender, blend the mixture well while still warm. This process homogenizes the base and promotes a smoother, creamier finished product.

**7** Transfer the base to your storage vessel and store in the refrigerator overnight. When you're ready to make ice cream, remove it from the refrigerator and again blend with an immersion blender until smooth and creamy.

**8** Pour the base into an ice cream maker and freeze according to the manufacturer's instructions.

**9** Once finished, store the ice cream in the freezer and resist the urge to open that door! A hard-scoop ice cream will need to set overnight.

**10** If you simply can't wait, you can certainly eat the ice cream right out of the machine; however, the consistency will be closer to soft-serve than hard-scoop.

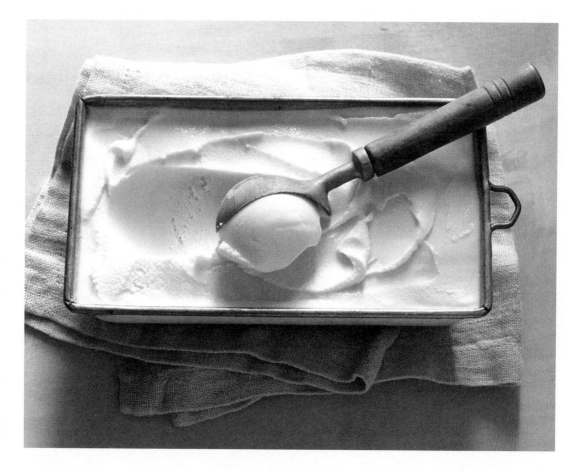

# RECIPES INSPIRED BY OTHER ICE CREAMS, DESSERTS & SNACKS

*LET'S START WITH THE SWEET SPOT*—the dessert and snack categories. From doughnuts and pastries to popcorn and pretzels, this section takes your favorite snack food and freeze-ifies it.

### THE ICE CREAM EPIPHANIES

The question I'm most frequently asked is "Where did you *come up* with this?" Inspiration for ice cream, thanks to its incredibly forgiving nature and adaptability, can come from just about anything, ranging from a piping hot dish of fresh pasta to the salty smell of a summer day at the beach.

I like to tell stories, and through ice cream I can channel those stories, transforming them into tasty, quietly captivating tales; it's a platform on which to parlay memories and share favorite moments, all while creating new ones.

# MALTESE PECAN

MAKES ABOUT 1 QUART *ICE CREAM*

Inspiration here came from a weekend trip to Charleston, South Carolina, where I was called in off the street and into the city's many candy shops by the aroma of slow-roasted pecans petrified in syrupy, crumbly praline. They were so irresistible, I found myself on more than one occasion skipping meals in favor of these sweet little pieces of southern comfort.

I didn't want to exactly plagiarize the praline, not for fear that I might not do it justice, but to create something that paid homage to Charleston's specialty. At Hay Rosie, our Tasting Room manager-cum-candy-and-baking-master Chrissy Ward set to work perfecting what I believe is the most cracklike commodity produced to date: Sea-Salted Chocolate-Covered Pecan Toffee (page 18).

**Blank Ice Cream Base (page 54)**

**½ cup malted milk powder**

**1½ cups Sea-Salted Chocolate-Covered Pecan Toffee (page 18)**

1 Prepare the blank base according to instructions.

2 When you're ready to make the ice cream, again blend the base with an immersion blender until smooth and creamy. Add the malted milk powder and continue blending until completely dissolved.

3 Pour into an ice cream maker and freeze according to the manufacturer's instructions. Once the ice cream is finished freezing, gently fold in the toffee pieces, store in an airtight container, and freeze overnight.

## MEET ITS MATCH
**Fernet & Coffee Caramel Ice Cream** *(page 159)*, **Honeyed Peanut Butter Sauce** *(page 25)* **& Bourbon Ganache** *(page 37)*, **Bananas Ferrari Ice Cream** *(page 62)*. **Or pair with just one big giant spoon.**

# SAGE CHOCOLATE CHIP

MAKES ABOUT 1 QUART *ICE CREAM*

Oh, mint chocolate chip, how I love you. But how did you manage to get the monopoly on American ice cream cabinets? Marcia, Marcia, Marcia—that's the mantra that comes to mind when I think about mint in the dessert world. Who decided it was the *only* herb worth a damn in a nonsavory dish? I decided to give mint a breather and put sage in the game. Turns out, we've got another star player: sweet, herbaceous, and a natural complement to homemade, melt-in-your-mouth Chocolate Snaps (page 20).

2 sprigs sage

1¾ cups heavy cream

Blank Ice Cream Base (page 54)

Chocolate Snaps (page 20)

### MEET ITS MATCH

Salty Buttered Honey Ice Cream *(page 80)*, Marshmallow Whiff *(page 36)*, pistachio, coconut, fig jam. A scoop between two amaretti cookies makes a nutty, fragrant ice cream sandwich.

1. Gently bruise the sage sprigs either by using the unsharpened side of a kitchen knife or simply by pressing them between the heels of your hands (this releases all those wonderful oils and aromatics). In a small saucepan over medium heat, add the sage to the cream. Bring to a gentle simmer for 5 to 7 minutes. Remove the sage and cool the cream completely.

2. Use the infused cream to prepare the blank base according to the standard instructions.

3. Store in the refrigerator overnight. When you're ready to make the ice cream, blend the base with an immersion blender until smooth and creamy.

4. Pour the base into an ice cream maker and freeze according to the manufacturer's instructions. Once the ice cream is finished freezing, gently fold in the Chocolate Snaps. Store in an airtight container and freeze overnight. To serve, sandwich a scoop between chewy Sage Chocolate Chip Cookies (page 149) for a sweet, herbaceous, and super delicious spin.

## MEET ITS MATCH

**Strawberry Pop-Tart Ice Cream** (*page 70*),
**The Wise Pumpkin Ice Cream** (*page 91*),
**India Pale Ice Cream** (*page 160*). Or top this off
with **Marshmallow Whiff** (*page 36*) and **Tequila
Lime Curd** (*page 178*) for a faux frozen margarita.

# LEMON BAR *ICE CREAM* MAKES ABOUT 1 QUART

I've always been oddly obsessed with lemon bars. I'm not talking about anything fancy—not some fresh-from-the-bakery, elevated, or overstylized versions. I'm talking those straight-outta-the-box, mix-and-make, bizarrely chewy, puckeringly tart and humble squares of non-pie.

Rather than chucking hunks of lemon bars into a blank base, I wanted to mimic the classic confections. And while I absolved the boxed lemon bar mix of its responsibilities, I maintained the general idea.

Fresh lemon curd is folded into a confectioners' sugar–flavored base, because if there's one thing a lemon bar isn't complete without, it's that signature dusting of snowy powder across its top.

5 teaspoons cornstarch

1³/₄ cups whole milk, divided

1³/₄ cups heavy cream

¹/₄ cup organic cane sugar

¹/₂ cup confectioners' sugar

5 tablespoons nonfat dry milk

Lemon Curd (page 28)

1 In a medium bowl, combine the starch with 3 tablespoons of the whole milk and whisk until smooth. Set aside.

2 In a nonreactive saucepan over medium heat, combine the cream, sugars, nonfat dry milk, and the remaining whole milk. Whisk assertively and frequently to ensure that the dry ingredients are well incorporated and no lumps remain.

3 In the meantime, prepare an ice bath in which to transfer your finished product by filling a large glass bowl with ice.

4 Once the base reaches a boil, reduce the heat and simmer for 4 to 5 minutes.

5 Add the starch-and-milk mixture and cook for 1 minute, stirring constantly with a rubber spatula. Remove from the heat and pour into a storage vessel set over your ice bath. (I typically use a glass Pyrex bowl with a cover, as the base will need to be stored after cooking, but a zip-top bag works well also.)

6 Using an immersion blender, blend the mixture well while still warm.

7 Store in the refrigerator overnight. When you're ready to make the ice cream, again blend the mixture with an immersion blender until smooth and creamy.

8 Pour into an ice cream maker and freeze according to the manufacturer's instructions.

9 Once the ice cream is finished freezing, package it by alternating layers of ice cream and pockets of Lemon Curd. You don't want to fold or stir, as the curd will churn into the ice cream. Store in an airtight container and freeze overnight.

# BANANAS FERRARI

MAKES ABOUT 1 QUART *ICE CREAM*

I've never liked banana-flavored things. Those little banana-shaped Runts? Their only real use to me was as a prop snack for my Ninja Turtle action figures. And while I do enjoy bananas, I only do so when they're exceptionally ripe and browning, possibly crossing into a realm that other people might call inedible or at least undesirable.

This flavor is influenced by that burnt caramel, super-ripe, buttery flavor of Bananas Foster—the only banana dish I ever loved. Bananas cooked long in nutty brown butter, studded with crunchy chunks of malty, salty goodness; it's addictive in the most authentically banana way.

2 ripe bananas

1 tablespoon butter

2 tablespoons muscovado sugar

Blank Ice Cream Base (page 54)

1¼ cups Malted Salted Toffee (page 21) pieces

### MEET ITS MATCH

**Mexican Muscovado Caramel Sauce** *(page 34)*, **Marshmallow Whiff** *(page 36)*, **Honeyed Peanut Butter Sauce** *(page 25)*, **Strawberry Pop-Tart Ice Cream** *(page 70)*, **Melted Ice Cream French Toast** *(page 136)*.

1  Slice the bananas into ¼" pieces and set aside.

2  Cook the butter in a light-colored saucepan over medium heat until browned. It should smell nutty and start to produce brown flecks. Add the reserved banana slices and sugar. Cook until the bananas brown and begin to fall apart. At this point you should be able to easily mash them with the back of a fork.

3  Transfer to a blender (or use an immersion blender) and puree the banana mixture. Allow it to cool completely.

4  Prepare the blank base according to instructions.

5  When you're ready to make the ice cream, again blend the base with an immersion blender until smooth and creamy. Add the banana puree and continue blending until completely integrated.

6  Pour into an ice cream maker and freeze according to the manufacturer's instructions. Once the ice cream is finished freezing, gently fold in the Malted Salted Toffee. Store in an airtight container and freeze overnight. Serve with Coffee Caramel Sauce (page 30) and Sea-Salted Chocolate-Covered Pecan Toffee (page 18) for the sunniest breakfast-style sundae.

## MEET ITS MATCH

Any item that chocolate would love. Top or swirl through with Mint Cherry Compote *(page 26)*, Lemon Curd *(page 28)*, Honeyed Peanut Butter Sauce *(page 25)*, or Simple Strawberry Jam *(page 43)*. Serve to the most intense chocolate-lover in your life.

# CHOCOLATE SORBET

The whole sorbet thing never quite did it for me. But as the public interest evolved, I figured I'd have to get with the times. Chocolate seemed like the natural place to start, since I could wrap my head around the science: Cocoa butter supplants some of the creaminess lost when excluding the butterfat so critical to crafting an ice cream.

There's also a comprehensible reason to omit dairy to achieve a dense and authentic flavor: Milk dilutes what would otherwise be a bold, complex, overpowering dark chocolate jolt to the taste buds.

The shocking result is the sole reason that you won't find any chocolate ice cream recipes in this book. They could never quite compete with the satisfaction factor of this incredibly decadent, ultra-creamy sorbet. So if you're still holding out for the sans-lactose section, I suggest you start here.

2½ cups water, divided
¾ cup firmly packed dark brown sugar
½ cup organic cane sugar
⅔ cup unsweetened cocoa powder
¾ cup finely chopped bittersweet chocolate
1 vanilla bean, scraped
Dash of salt

1   In a small saucepan over medium heat, combine 1½ cups of the water, the sugars, and the cocoa. Whisk until well integrated and smooth. Bring to a boil and cook for 1 to 2 minutes.

2   Remove from the heat and add the chocolate, vanilla bean seeds, salt, and the remaining 1 cup water. Using an immersion blender, puree the mixture until smooth. Age the mixture in the refrigerator until fully cooled. While it isn't imperative that the mix be aged overnight, it is preferable.

3   When you're ready to make the sorbet, again blend the mixture with an immersion blender until smooth and creamy.

4   Pour into an ice cream maker and freeze according to the manufacturer's instructions. Once the sorbet is finished freezing, store it in an airtight container and freeze overnight.

## SUGGESTED RIFFS

This black beauty is super customizable, which is another reason to love it so much.

**MINT CACAO NIB SORBET:** Add ½ teaspoon peppermint extract and ¼ cup crushed cacao nibs.

**CHOCOLATE-COVERED ORANGE SORBET:** Add ½ teaspoon orange essential oil and the zest of 1 orange.

**BUMPY BQE:** Layer in pouches of Marshmallow Whiff (page 36) and handfuls of smoked almonds for a scoop that can soothe the most maddening of Brooklyn traffic situations.

**COCO-RETTO CHOCOLATE:** Add ¼ cup toasted shredded coconut and ½ teaspoon almond extract.

# SRIRACHA POPCORN

*ICE CREAM*

I love popcorn—it's got that whole blank canvas thing that makes ice cream so much fun to me, but in the crunchy, salty column of the snack category. In particular, I love when it's doused in spicy, vinegary sriracha. But being a bit heavy-handed on the hot sauce, I sometimes make my popcorn far too soggy.

Once I realized I could make flakes of the stuff, it dawned on me that this was also the key to turning my midnight snack into an ice cream flavor.

Heat-seekers are often advised to drink a glass of milk with something spicy to neutralize the burn. This ice cream first serves up the punch and then quickly provides the cooling effect, not only from the obvious fact that it's frozen, but also from the dairy base.

It's important in this recipe not to use buttered popcorn, as the oils and flavorings can create a greasy ice cream. My preference is to pop kernels on the stovetop just before infusing, but you can also use bagged popcorn from the grocery store. Just be sure it's not loaded with oil and flavorings—the more natural, the better. If you're using bagged or prepopped corn, spread it over a baking pan in a thin layer and toast for 5 minutes at 220°F in the oven before infusing.

**3 tablespoons sriracha**

**2 cups freshly popped fat-free popcorn (not movie theater popcorn)**

**2¼ cups heavy cream**

**Blank Ice Cream Base (page 54)**

1. Line a baking sheet with parchment paper. Preheat the oven to 220°F. Using an offset spatula, spread the sriracha in a very thin layer across the parchment. Dehydrate the sriracha in the oven for about an hour, or until entirely dry. Allow to cool completely. At this point, it should peel or scrape off the parchment. Place the sriracha in a plastic bag and crush it into a powder. Set aside.

2. Begin with freshly popped corn, still warm. If you don't have fresh popcorn, you can toast bagged popcorn for 5 minutes in the oven at 200°F, or until the aroma of popcorn is noticeable. The fat-free popcorn is important as it won't have the oil that standard popcorn does, which creates a greasiness in the finished ice cream.

*(RECIPE CONTINUES)*

3  In a medium saucepan over medium heat, add the popcorn to the cream. Bring to a low simmer for 3 to 5 minutes. Using a mesh strainer set over a bowl, strain the liquid, pressing to ensure that you get as much of the flavored cream as possible. A bit of popcorn pulp may come through, but that's okay—it's delicious! Reserve the remaining solids for Popcorn Pudding (page 139). Allow the cream to cool completely.

4  You will lose some cream to absorption, so measure your remaining cream and add as needed to return to 1¾ cups of cream total.

5  Prepare the blank base according to standard instructions, but use the infused cream and decrease the sugar to ¼ cup.

6  Store in the refrigerator overnight. When you're ready to make the ice cream, again blend the mixture with an immersion blender until smooth and creamy.

7  Pour into an ice cream maker and freeze according to the manufacturer's instructions.

8  Just before the ice cream is finished churning, sprinkle in the sriracha powder and allow the beater to distribute the flakes. Adding the sriracha too early will rehydrate it and cause streaks of sriracha rather than flakes.

9  Store in an airtight container and freeze overnight.

**MEET ITS MATCH**
Honeyed Peanut Butter Sauce (page 25), toasted coconut, and Malted Hot Fudge (page 35) with a sprinkle of cinnamon; the stroke of midnight

# PRETZEL HONEY MUSTARD

**MAKES ABOUT 1 QUART** *ICE CREAM*

It took me an awfully long time to come around on condiments—for most of my life, not even a chicken nugget could be tainted by the allure of some saucy sidecar.

And then one day, I accidentally dug my hand into a friend's bag of honey mustard–flavored pretzels. With my attention elsewhere, I suddenly found my mouth filled with a spicy-sweet, tangy, and totally addictive flavor that I'd never before experienced.

From then on, I was a honey mustard maniac. And when I started tinkering with ice creams, naturally I wanted to shoehorn this typically savory stuff into a scoop. The pretzel base is a perfect host for the sweet and spicy sauce swirled throughout.

**1 cup mini pretzels**
**2¼ cups heavy cream**
**Blank Ice Cream Base (page 54)**
**Honey Mustard Swirl (page 31)**

### MEET ITS MATCH
**Salt & Sand Ice Cream** *(page 88)*, **Brown Sugar Sour Cream Softer-Serve** *(page 108)*, **Roasted Cherry Chocolate Snap Ice Cream** *(page 86)*; baseball games and cheap beer

1 In a medium saucepan over medium heat, add the pretzels to the cream. Bring to a low simmer for 3 to 5 minutes. Using a mesh strainer set over a bowl, strain the liquid, pressing through to ensure that you get as much of the flavored cream as possible. A bit of pretzel pulp may come through, but that's okay—it's delicious!

2 You will lose some cream to absorption, so measure your remaining cream and add as needed to return to 1¾ cups of cream total.

3 Prepare the blank base according to standard instructions, but use the infused cream and reduce the sugar to ¼ cup.

4 Store in the refrigerator overnight. When you're ready to make the ice cream, again blend the mixture with an immersion blender until smooth and creamy.

5 Pour into an ice cream maker and freeze according to the manufacturer's instructions.

6 Once the ice cream is finished freezing, package it by alternating layers of ice cream and pockets of Honey Mustard Swirl. You don't want to fold or stir, as the swirl will churn into the ice cream. Store in an airtight container and freeze overnight.

# STRAWBERRY POP-TART

MAKES ABOUT 1 QUART *ICE CREAM*

At some point in my life, I became *possessed* by the idea of pristine Pop-Tarts. Perhaps the pretty white frosting spackled with rainbow-colored "sprinkles" (that really aren't sprinkles at all) appealed to my vanity. Or maybe it's the fact that not many whole, undamaged examples seem to actually exist; the relative rarity of a pair of pastries that survives its transit is so elusive, it had me totally entranced.

As a tween, I was once reduced to tears because my strawberry frosted snack hit the floor, a precious corner of my pie's crust separating from the whole. I refused to accept my poor sister's attempts to appease me by offering its less abused but still inadmissibly imperfect twin. I can't possibly explain this phenomenon, but to this very day I find myself unsettled by the sight of even a slightly damaged toaster pastry.

I made this ice cream for that crazed 12-year-old so troubled by her marred treat. And I was able to finally enjoy the flavor of a strawberry toaster pastry, safe in the knowledge that in this iteration, there's very little chance of a cosmetically compromised outcome. Call me crazy—I certainly would—but I can feel the younger me beaming at its incorruptibility.

1 prepared piecrust
2¼ cups heavy cream
Blank Ice Cream Base (page 54)
1 cup rainbow sprinkles
Simple Strawberry Jam (page 43)

1. Preheat the oven and bake the prepared piecrust according to the package instructions. While still warm, break the piecrust into pieces, reserving 1 cup.

2. To infuse the cream, in a medium saucepan over medium heat, add the piecrust to the cream. Bring to a low simmer for 3 to 5 minutes. Using a mesh strainer set over a bowl, strain the liquid, pressing through to ensure that you get as much of the flavored cream as possible. A bit of piecrust pulp may come through, but that's okay—it's delicious!

3. You will lose some cream to absorption, so measure your remaining cream and add as needed to return to 1¾ cups of cream total.

4. Prepare the blank base according to standard instructions, but use the infused cream and reduce the sugar to ¼ cup.

*(RECIPE CONTINUES)*

5   Store in the refrigerator overnight. When you're ready to make the ice cream, again blend the mixture with an immersion blender until smooth and creamy.

6   Pour into an ice cream maker and freeze according to the manufacturer's instructions. Just before the ice cream is finished churning, pour in the sprinkles and allow the beater to distribute.

7   Once the ice cream is frozen, package it by alternating layers of ice cream and pockets of strawberry jam. You don't want to fold or stir, as the swirl will churn into the ice cream. Store in an airtight container and freeze overnight.

## MEET ITS MATCH

**Salty Buttered Honey Ice Cream** *(page 80)*, **Honeyed Peanut Butter Sauce** *(page 25)* **and Bourbon Ganache** *(page 37)*, **Grape-Nuts Ice Cream** *(page 96)*, **White Chocolate Enchanted Shell** *(page 39)*, **Better-Than-Buttermilk Biscuits** *(page 132)*; **obsessive-compulsive behavior**

# PBBG ICE CREAM

MAKES ABOUT 1 QUART

You know those weird frozen peanut butter and jelly sandwiches that are supposed to be crust-free but in actuality have a strange type of crust all their own? I'm crazy for them.

And so I almost lost my mind when I went to grab a box for an impending road trip and found that they'd introduced a new model: Peanut Butter & Honey. Later on, when Emily and I shared a few after a decidedly long day of driving, we poured a bit of bourbon into our motel-issued coffee mugs. The pairing was perfection, but we decided a bit of chocolate would be a welcome enhancement.

Unfortunately, without fresh ganache on hand, we had to settle for a vending machine chocolate bar. But what you have here is the elevated ice cream equivalent of that particular road trip picnic.

## MEET ITS MATCH

**Marshmallow Whiff** *(page 36)*, **Pretzel Honey Mustard Ice Cream** *(page 69)*, **Bananas Ferrari Ice Cream** *(page 62)*, **Oatmeal Cinnamon Ice Cream** *(page 97)*, **Grape-Nuts Ice Cream** *(page 96)*; your favorite travel buddy

**Blank Ice Cream Base (page 54)**
**Seeds scraped from 1 vanilla bean**
**Honeyed Peanut Butter Sauce (page 25)**
**Bourbon Ganache (page 37)**

1  Prepare the blank base according to instructions.

2  When you're ready to make the ice cream, again blend the base with an immersion blender until smooth and creamy. Add the vanilla bean seeds and continue blending until completely dissolved.

3  Pour into an ice cream maker and freeze according to the manufacturer's instructions. Once the ice cream is frozen, package it by alternating layers of ice cream and pockets of Honeyed Peanut Butter Sauce and Bourbon Ganache. (If your sauce has been in the fridge, it's best to remove it about 30 minutes prior.) You don't want to fold or stir, as the sauce can churn into the ice cream. Store in an airtight container and freeze overnight.

# OVALTINE & OREO ICE CREAM

MAKES ABOUT 1 QUART *(AKA AFTER-SCHOOL SNACK)*

The only thing more thrilling than the last bell of the school day was what welcomed me when I got home. This malty milk drink matched with the classic sandwich cookies was a rare treat, but one that likely informed my later love for Ovaltine's slightly grown-up and less sugary cousin, malted milk.

**Blank Ice Cream Base (page 54)**

**1/2 cup Ovaltine powder**

**1 cup crushed sandwich cookies**

## MEET ITS MATCH

**A drizzle of Ginger Hibiscus Syrup** *(page 27)* **cuts through the sweetness of the Ovaltine. Pair with a scoop of Strawberry Pop-Tart Ice Cream** *(page 70)* **for a supermarket-inspired sundae.**

1. Prepare the blank base according to instructions.

2. When you're ready to make the ice cream, again blend the base with an immersion blender until smooth and creamy. Add the Ovaltine and continue blending until completely dissolved.

3. Pour into an ice cream maker and freeze according to the manufacturer's instructions. Once the ice cream is finished freezing, gently fold in the cookie pieces. Store in an airtight container and freeze overnight.

# RECIPES INSPIRED BY DINNERS, DATES, AND OTHER DISHES

*IT SEEMS RELATIVELY OBVIOUS* to turn desserts into ice cream, so where we're coming from is slightly less mentally challenging than where we're going. This next section will require a little bit of imagination and some mind-bending of the rules that we've so long accepted as our confectionary credo.

So let's do it together. Let's buck the system. Let's question authority. Let's venture into undiscovered territory. Because at the end of the day, we're not introducing new flavor combinations; these are ice creams inspired by dishes we already know and love, dishes that we know *work*—we're just meeting them under different circumstances.

Consider this the *Missed Connection* section of the ice cream cabinet, the ice-cream-ification of things that would otherwise never get the chance to be someone's favorite frozen treat.

# FINOCCHIO E LA CAPRA
MAKES ABOUT
1 QUART
## (FENNEL & THE GOAT) *ICE CREAM*

There are meals, and then there are *experiences*. The kind that make you put down your fork and close your eyes and wonder if you'll ever need to eat again, because you may have just uncovered the epicurean equivalent of beating the game. No need to persist because there are no higher levels. You've saved the princess. You are the winner.

For my 27th birthday, my wife, Emily, surprised me with dinner at Mario Batali's West Village institution, Babbo Ristorante. A variety of dishes decorated our starched white tablecloth, expertly coursed by our server and thoughtfully paired by a sommelier: arugula salads, cheeses and fresh fish, seared duck, and—being autumn—a maple pumpkin cheesecake for dessert that still finds its way into my dreams. But the pièce de résistance, the dish for which I have returned dozens of times over the years that followed, was the Goat Cheese Tortelloni with Dried Orange and Wild Fennel Pollen.

It was the first time I'd ever tasted the ingestible precious metal that is fennel pollen. Have you had this magic dust? Incredible. As a finishing spice, it's delicately floral with hints of licorice, honey, and citrus and undertones of what I can only describe as sweet marshmallow and exotic vanilla. It is nothing short of ethereal.

When I finished the dish and rejoined my earthly surroundings, I immediately began thinking how it would lend itself to ice cream. The creamy, tangy goat cheese and zest of orange against that sweet, heady, and floral fennel pollen wrapped up in a frozen scoop—it's pure sorcery.

Because fennel pollen is such a delicate spice, it's best to add it just before spinning the ice cream to preserve its flavor and perfume.

Enjoy, and attempt not to float away with happiness. . . .

### MEET ITS MATCH
The Wise Pumpkin Ice Cream (*page 91*), Bananas Ferrari Ice Cream (*page 62*), Mint Cherry Mascarpone Ice Cream (*page 84*), Lemon Bar Ice Cream (*page 61*), or Simple Strawberry Jam (*page 43*). Serve over piping hot fresh pasta, mixed in for a creamy-cool sauce.

Blank Ice Cream Base (page 54)

¾ cup pea-size chunks goat cheese

1 teaspoon fennel pollen

1½ teaspoons orange zest

1 Prepare the blank base according to instructions.

2 When you're ready to make the ice cream, again blend the base with an immersion blender until smooth and creamy. Add the cheese in batches and continue blending until completely integrated. Finally, blend in the fennel pollen and orange zest. Adding them just prior to freezing will help maintain their aromatics.

3 Pour into an ice cream maker and freeze according to the manufacturer's instructions. Once the ice cream is finished freezing, store in an airtight container and freeze overnight.

## ROCKY ROAD TRIP

# NEW JERSEY

### ⊤ RICH'S ICE CREAM II, TOMS RIVER

Route 37 in Emily's hometown of Toms River is a heavily traveled main road, but hardly a 10-minute drive to the summertime destination of Seaside Heights, it's still perfectly demonstrative of the area's beach-town spirit.

Rich's II's soft-serve is some of the densest, creamiest, and most palate-coatingly pleasurable that I have come across, and on a post-shore summer night, sunburnt and still in sandy flip-flops, there's no place I'd rather be.

Rich's serves both hard and soft ice creams, but their creative shakes and "blend-in" desserts are distinctive specialties. The building is buttoned with colorful homemade signs like merit badges, describing and illustrating each signature, like Lemon Meringue Pie (vanilla ice cream with vanilla mousse, lemon pie filling, and graham cracker crumbs) or Rice Pudding flurries or the Cone-oli (a cone of vanilla soft-serve layered with cannoli cream and cannoli shells and topped with chocolate crunch crumbs).

**WHAT I'M HAVING:** As it's one of her few favorite sweet spots, first I'm ordering Emily a tall chocolate malted with cake crunchies. Then I'm having the seasonal flurry all to myself.

# FETA TOMATO SWIRL

MAKES ABOUT 1 QUART  *ICE CREAM*

Yes, *that* feta and *that* tomato. This dish is loosely based on a salad my mother-in-law makes in the summertime. It's one of my favorite bowls on the buffet at her backyard barbecues, and usually I find myself hovering over it, hoping to intercept other guests' attempts to access.

It got me thinking about the sweetness of tomatoes—a piece of produce that for some reason we never give credit for being a fruit. Caramelizing them here with a little bit of brown sugar draws depth of flavor at once bright and deeply sweet. The feta is a tangy counterpoint, and as nicely as they play together in a salad, you haven't had this pairing done right until you've invited them over for dessert.

Best not to force this flavor when tomatoes aren't in season. The freshness factor is critical to the caramel, so if you've selected wintertime tomatoes that are more water than substance, you'll find that the outcome is hardly worth the effort.

## MEET ITS MATCH

**Sage Chocolate Chip Ice Cream** (*page 58*), **Mexican Muscovado Caramel Sauce** (*page 34*); chunks of watermelon and torn mint leaves for an ultimate summertime salad

**Blank Ice Cream Base (page 54)**
**¹⁄₂ cup pea-size chunks feta cheese**
**Tomato Caramel Sauce (page 33)**

1 Prepare the blank base according to instructions.

2 When you're ready to make the ice cream, again blend with an immersion blender until smooth and creamy. Add the cheese in batches and continue blending until completely integrated.

3 Pour the mixture into an ice cream maker and freeze according to the manufacturer's instructions.

4 Once the ice cream is finished freezing, package it by alternating layers of ice cream and pockets of Tomato Caramel Sauce. Be careful not to fold or stir, as the swirl will churn into the ice cream. Store in an airtight container and freeze overnight.

# SALTY BUTTERED HONEY

MAKES ABOUT 1 QUART *ICE CREAM*

In the pastoral neighborhood of Carroll Gardens in Brooklyn, there are plenty of restaurants that could inspire ice cream flavors. But it is a bistro called Buttermilk Channel that can take credit for my leasing an apartment around the corner.

And while their brunch is not to be missed (bourbon-pecan French toast, people) and the dinner is divine (two words: *duck meatloaf*), what really captured my attention was the first thing brought to the table: pert, delicate, freshly baked popovers drizzled with local honey and decorated with flakes of crunchy sea salt.

Using good butter and quality honey, this ice cream emulates that fresh popover flavor, and, of course, the indispensable salt flakes completely solidify its perfection.

Be aware that this ice cream can be tricky. Because of the addition of melted butter, it's easy to overchurn, so keep an eye on the ice cream as it spins. It may not take quite as long as your manufacturer's instructions suggest.

### MEET ITS MATCH

Cinnamon, fruit-based ice creams, your favorite marmalade, predinner popovers, apple pie, freshly baked biscuits. Swap a scoop in place of vanilla for the strawberry shortcake you never knew you were missing.

5 teaspoons cornstarch

1¾ cups whole milk, divided

2 tablespoons butter, melted

1¼ cups heavy cream

½ cup honey

5 tablespoons nonfat dry milk

½ teaspoon flaked sea salt

1. In a small bowl, combine the starch with 3 tablespoons of the milk and whisk until smooth. Set aside.

2. In a nonreactive saucepan over medium heat, combine the butter, cream, honey, and nonfat dry milk. Whisk until well incorporated. Add the remaining whole milk and bring to a boil, whisking frequently.

3. In the meantime, prepare an ice bath in which to transfer your finished product by filling a large glass bowl with ice.

4. Once the base reaches a boil, reduce the heat and simmer for 4 to 5 minutes.

5. Add the reserved starch-and-milk mixture and cook for 1 minute, stirring constantly with a rubber spatula. Remove from the heat and pour into a storage vessel set over your ice bath. (I typically use a glass Pyrex bowl with a cover.)

6  Using an immersion blender, blend the mixture well while still warm. This process homogenizes the base and promotes a smoother, creamier finished product.

7  Store in the refrigerator overnight. When you're ready to make the ice cream, remove the mixture from the refrigerator and again blend with an immersion blender until smooth and creamy.

8  Pour into an ice cream maker and freeze according to the manufacturer's instructions.

9  Once finished, store the ice cream in your freezer and resist the urge to open that door! A hard-scoop ice cream will need to set overnight.

10  If you simply can't wait, you can certainly eat the ice cream right out of the machine; however, the consistency will be closer to soft-serve than hard-scoop.

## ROCKY ROAD TRIP

# CONNECTICUT

### ⊤ FERRIS ACRES CREAMERY, NEWTOWN

This is my home-field-advantage farm. When I head back to Connecticut for any period of time or purpose, upon wheels down I am darting directly to this idyllic dairy farm situated in the back roads of Newtown, on the aptly named Sugar Street. There you can commune with the cows, grazing on the fruits of their labor as they lazily return disinterested glances, enjoying their own grassy snack break from the lush green pasture surrounding the iconic red barn. This is the New England ice cream I grew up with.

In a rare double threat, they have both exemplary rich, perfectly formulated homemade hard scoop and the purest, most fully flavored soft-serve to satisfy either hankering. If I had to pick my happiest place on Earth, eating ice cream amongst Ferris Acres' aloof clique of cows would probably be it.

**WHAT I'M HAVING:** Their homemade ice creams truly do cover the something-for-everyone catalogue, and the special and seasonal flavors like Caramel Apple Pie are exceptional. But my go-to jam? A cup of Raspberry Swirl Chunk on the bottom and, on top, Cow Trax (vanilla ice cream with alternating peanut butter and caramel swirls, studded with tiny, soft chocolate chips). Or stuff those flavors into one of their to-die-for ice cream cakes and I am totally done for.

# CACIO E PEPE

**MAKES ABOUT 1 QUART** *ICE CREAM*

Ah, honeymoons. The romance! The passion! The wedded bliss! The bowls and bowls of handmade pasta!

During our neo-nuptial retreat, my wife and I spent 3 days in Rome, a jaunt in which I made it a point to sample gelati from just about every vendor that offered it to me, and she to create a catalogue of the classic Roman pasta dish, *Cacio e Pepe*, from joints all over the city. Needless to say, it was a very, very *full* trip.

Upon return, when our respective withdrawals kicked in hard, it seemed only fitting to find a way to marry our two favorite take-aways. In the midst of our collective post-travel sorrow, I made my second vow to her: to transform the dish into something that might stem the pain of her sudden stateside pasta deprivation.

### MEET ITS MATCH

No need to adjust your eyesight—that *is* ice cream served over spaghetti. As this flavor melts into the dish, it becomes a perfectly creamy sauce for your pasta dinner. Or try Salty Buttered Honey Ice Cream *(page 80)*, Simple Strawberry Jam *(page 43)*, a drizzle of balsamic vinegar, Mediterranean sunsets, and crusty toasted bread

½ cup grated Grana Padano cheese
**Blank Ice Cream Base (page 54)**
½ tablespoon cracked black pepper

1. Place the cheese in a heatproof bowl. Prepare the blank base according to instructions. While hot, pour it over the cheese and whisk vigorously.

2. Using a cheesecloth, strain out any cheese not melted into the base.

3. Store the mixture in the refrigerator overnight. When you're ready to make the ice cream, again blend with an immersion blender until smooth and creamy. Add the pepper and blend until well integrated.

4. Pour into an ice cream maker and freeze according to the manufacturer's instructions.

5. Store in an airtight container and freeze overnight.

6. To make the pasta dish, allow a scoop to melt over a fresh tangle of pasta for a unique take on the dinner dish.

# MINT CHERRY MASCARPONE

*ICE CREAM*

Mint is a classic lamb complement. Mint jelly, however, has always just sounded . . . well, odd. So when I found the inspiration for this ice cream on a restaurant menu, I read the description, thinking *Now that is something I can get on board with.* The dish arrived, grilled lamb garnished with mint pesto and surrounded by small dunes of cherry mascarpone cream through which to drag each forkful. Sorry, mint jelly, but may I suggest moving to the Jell-O section?

In its frozen form, the creamy mascarpone cheese base provides a lush backdrop for the tart, herbaceous cherry sauce swirled throughout. Infusing the cherries with fistfuls of fresh mint while they cook results in a bright herbal burst and beautiful green flecks against the deep red. Because this recipe uses dried cherries, you can make this ice cream all year long.

## MEET ITS MATCH

Dark chocolate, toasted almond, ginger, or brown sugar ice creams, a citrus sorbet, a drizzle of balsamic syrup. Add a scoop to a glass of good bourbon for a smashing julep.

**Blank Ice Cream Base (page 54)**
**1/2 cup mascarpone, at room temperature**
**Mint Cherry Compote (page 26)**

1  Prepare the blank base according to instructions.

2  When you're ready to make the ice cream, again blend the base with an immersion blender until smooth and creamy. Add the cheese in batches and continue blending until completely integrated.

3  Pour into an ice cream maker and freeze according to the manufacturer's instructions.

4  Once the ice cream is finished freezing, package it by alternating layers of ice cream and pockets of Mint Cherry Compote. Store in an airtight container and freeze overnight.

# SEASONAL INSPIRATIONS

*IN MY EARLY TWENTIES*, I moved to Southern California. I thought I'd take the opportunity to brag to all of my East Coast friends and family about the ceaseless sunny days, the everlasting summer, and all the perks that came along with a West Coast address. But after the first full year, I found myself in a chair at a local tattoo parlor, the artist tracing a stencil on my arm illustrating the progression of summer into fall, winter, and then spring. With my fresh ink, I went home and ate my words—I desperately missed each Northeast season.

Eventually I moved to New York, where I proceeded to bitch and moan with the best of 'em about the cold, the rain, the relentless winter. But while our grass may not be greener, per se, I wouldn't trade that annual evolution.

These flavors are little frozen odes to my appreciation of the seasons—sometimes purely in theory, other times thanks to ingredients that we appreciate far more as a result of their absence the rest of the year.

# ROASTED CHERRY CHOCOLATE SNAP ICE CREAM

During one early summer morning at the market, a mountain of fresh cherries caught me completely off guard. While it threw off both my plan and my budget for the day, I emptied the bank and cleaned them out of the fresh stash of rotund New York State cherries. I then promptly scrapped the plan for the day and began the process of slow-roasting those beauties; I wanted absolutely nothing—other than vanilla bean and a little brown sugar—to interfere with their flavor. But the vibrant cherry swirl begged for a little texture and bittersweet chocolate, so I happily obliged.

**2 cups fresh cherries, pitted and stemmed (frozen cherries can work here as well)**

**¼ cup balsamic vinegar**

**½ cup brown sugar**

**Blank Ice Cream Base (page 54)**

**Seeds scraped from 1 vanilla bean (Tahitian, if possible)**

**1 cup Chocolate Snaps (page 20)**

### MEET ITS MATCH

**Lemon Bar Ice Cream** (page 61), **Sage Chocolate Chip Ice Cream** (page 58), **Savannah Sweet Tea Ice Cream** (page 165), **Basil Julep Ice Cream** (page 163).

1. Line a baking sheet with parchment paper.

2. Preheat the oven to 425°F. In a bowl, combine the cherries, vinegar, and sugar. Spread on the baking sheet. Roast for about 30 minutes, or until the cherries begin to release their juices. Allow to cool completely.

3. Prepare the blank base according to instructions.

4. When you're ready to make the ice cream, again blend the base with an immersion blender until smooth and creamy. Add the vanilla bean seeds and blend until incorporated.

5. Pour into an ice cream maker and freeze according to the manufacturer's instructions. Once the ice cream is finished freezing, gently fold in the cherries and Chocolate Snaps. Store in an airtight container and freeze overnight.

# SALT & SAND

MAKES ABOUT 1 QUART  *ICE CREAM*

The idea behind Salt & Sand came from a day at the beach, at the end of which it's common to have both of those things in your hair, your clothes, your shoes, and even your teeth. That crunchy saline sensation is inextricably linked to so many summer experiences that I'm particularly fond of.

The key is to fold the sugar and salt into the finished ice cream *very* carefully. If you overdo it, both will dissolve into the mix, and while the flavor will still be pleasant, you'll lose the texture that is so integral to the idea and the enjoyment.

**Blank Ice Cream Base (page 54)**
**¹/₂ teaspoon flaky sea salt, such as Maldon**
**1 cup muscovado sugar**

### MEET ITS MATCH
**Bananas Ferrari Ice Cream** *(page 62)*, **Feta Tomato Swirl Ice Cream** *(page 78)*, **Pretzel Honey Mustard Ice Cream** *(page 69)*; **a tall glass of lemonade and a day at the beach**

1. Prepare the blank base according to instructions.

2. When you're ready to make the ice cream, again blend the base with an immersion blender until smooth and creamy.

3. Pour into an ice cream maker and freeze according to the manufacturer's instructions. Once the ice cream is finished freezing, gently fold in the sea salt. As you package it, alternate layers of ice cream with shallow pockets of the sugar. The idea is to ensure that it doesn't dissolve into liquid but, rather, maintains a crunchiness.

4. Store in an airtight container and freeze overnight.

# SEÑORITA PEPITAS

MAKES ABOUT 1 QUART *ICE CREAM*

Pumpkin ice cream is practically a plague in the fall. The world begins begging for the perennial flavor more and more prematurely each year. In the beer business, we were brewing pumpkin ales as early as July to sate the public's squash complex. And here's my dirty little secret: I'm part of the pumpkin problem. But in an effort to keep the patch from becoming overpopulated with the same cinnamon-laden patterns, I've tried to develop a few different iterations of ice creams grounded in the gourd.

When I was a kid, one of my favorite things about carving jack-o'-lanterns was roasting the seeds; "pepitas" just sounds more fun, so I prefer to call them by this alias now. And it seemed like with a spicy new moniker, they deserved their own ice cream flavor, so I created this non-pumpkin pumpkin ice cream, complete with a little kick.

## MEET ITS MATCH
**Oatmeal Cinnamon Ice Cream** (page 97), **Marshmallow Whiff** (page 36), **Chocolate Sorbet** (page 65); **White Chocolate Enchanted Shell** (page 39) and a drizzle of **Malted Hot Fudge** (page 35)

Blank Ice Cream Base (page 54)

$1/4$ teaspoon ground red pepper (adjust to $1/8$ teaspoon if you're on the shy side of hot stuff!)

$1\frac{1}{2}$ cups Spicy Pumpkin Seed Crunch (page 23)

1 Prepare the blank base according to instructions.

2 When you're ready to make the ice cream, again blend the base with an immersion blender until smooth and creamy. Add the pepper and blend until incorporated.

3 Pour into an ice cream maker and freeze according to the manufacturer's instructions. Once the ice cream is finished freezing, gently fold in the Spicy Pumpkin Seed Crunch pieces, store in an airtight container, and freeze overnight.

# THE WISE PUMPKIN

MAKES ABOUT 1 QUART *ICE CREAM*

Yet another riff on the pumpkin mania and, as it so happens, another pasta dish—this one from Frankie's 457 in Carroll Gardens, Brooklyn—a sweet potato and sage ravioli. There's something warm and cozy about the flavor of sage, something comforting and completely appropriate for autumn. Since Sage Chocolate Chip was already a staple, the decision to merge the flavors was simple.

But the name of this ice cream is perhaps my favorite of all. Whenever I hear someone say it out loud, I laugh a little inside, imagining a weathered old squash sitting up on that person's shoulder, his spectacles sliding low on his nonexistent nose, carrying a cane, with a few sprigs of the herb where its stem should be. He's a sage old soul (and *so* adorable), and a damn tasty one at that.

### MEET ITS MATCH
*Cacio e Pepe* Ice Cream *(page 83),* Oatmeal Cinnamon Ice Cream *(page 97);* crushed, salty smoked almonds and a drizzle of orange olive oil

**Sage Chocolate Chip Ice Cream (page 58)**
**1 cup pumpkin puree**
**Chocolate Snaps (page 20)**

1 Prepare the Sage Chocolate Chip Ice Cream, except when the mix has been removed from the stovetop, add the pumpkin puree and blend until smooth.

2 Age the mixture overnight. When you're ready to make the ice cream, again blend it with an immersion blender until smooth and creamy.

3 Pour into an ice cream maker and freeze according to the manufacturer's instructions. Once the ice cream is finished freezing, gently fold in the Chocolate Snaps. Store in an airtight container and freeze overnight.

# BOG CABIN *ICE CREAM*

I love New England. It's the kind of love that comes from growing up in a place and dying to get away, only to leave and realize there's a whole lot you actually owe to your hometown.

With this flavor, I wanted to pay tribute to my New England ancestry. Some of the most northeastern of novelties are cranberries and maple syrup, and there's just nothing better together. A little bit of ginger in the base gives the whole affair a decidedly yuletide effect, so I like to serve this during our annual open house.

**1³/₄ cups heavy cream**
**¹/₄" piece fresh ginger, crushed**
**Blank Ice Cream Base (page 54)**
**Maple-Molasses Cranberry Sauce (page 24)**

### MEET ITS MATCH

**Lemon Bar Ice Cream** *(page 61)*, **gingerbread, mulled red wine, orange zest; Melted Ice Cream Pancakes** *(page 134)* **or Melted Ice Cream French Toast** *(page 136)* **on Christmas morning.**

1. In a small saucepan over medium heat, combine the cream and ginger. Bring to a simmer and cook for 5 minutes. Remove from the heat and allow the ginger to steep for 30 minutes. Remove the solids.

2. Use the infused cream to prepare the blank base according to the standard instructions.

3. When you're ready to make the ice cream, again blend the base with an immersion blender until smooth and creamy.

4. Pour into an ice cream maker and freeze according to the manufacturer's instructions.

5. Once the ice cream is finished freezing, package it by alternating layers of ice cream and pockets of Maple-Molasses Cranberry Sauce. Store in an airtight container and freeze overnight.

# ICE CREAM FOR BREAKFAST

*EVERY MORNING, ACROSS OUR* great nation and in many others, people eat yogurt for breakfast. Which—let's be real—is glorified (and maybe ever so *slightly* healthier) ice cream.

French toast is basically just bread pudding. Pan*cakes*? Read the name, people! And doughnuts? Don't make me go there. What kind of licensed dietitian or anyone with a working knowledge of the Food Pyramid (past or present) would encourage you to fuel the rest of your day with this stuff?

In fact, I say we finally just call breakfast what it is: sunrise dessert.

Of course, just as I wouldn't recommend a daily doughnut, I don't purport that ice cream is a part of a regularly encouraged or balanced breakfast. But on birthdays and special occasions, I support—nay, I demand—its right to be welcomed at the breakfast table.

# DOUGHNUT YA LOVE COFFEE
MAKES ABOUT 1 QUART ## ICE CREAM (AKA THE FUZZ)

If anyone asks what comes second to ice cream for me (this is all hypothetical, right?), the answer is always easy and unequivocal—doughnuts.

The idea of coffee and doughnuts together calls to mind dinners at my grandparents' house, a white cardboard pastry box open in offering, the grown-ups entertaining steaming mugs and us kids hyped up on our budgeted doughnut bisections, hovering close by in hopes of being eventually allowed the other halves.

In Brooklyn, we're lucky enough to have access to Dough doughnuts, which are the kind of blow-your-mind mix of contemporary quality and comforting nostalgia that I've come to hope for in a doughnut. For this flavor, I've used their Café au Lait doughnut for fortified caffeine, but it also works well with classic glazed or cruller-style doughnuts and with just about any flavor of your favorite fritters.

### MEET ITS MATCH

**Salty Buttered Honey Ice Cream** (*page 80*), **PBBG Ice Cream** (*page 73*), **Oatmeal Cinnamon Ice Cream** (*page 97*). **Roasted Cherry Chocolate Snap Ice Cream** (*page 86*), **Grape-Nuts Ice Cream** (*page 96*). **Bananas Ferrari Ice Cream** (*page 62*) **with a drizzle of White Chocolate Enchanted Shell** (*page 39*).

**Blank Ice Cream Base (page 54)**
**2 doughnuts, cut or torn into small chunks**
**Coffee Caramel Sauce (page 30)**

1 Prepare the blank base according to instructions.

2 When you're ready to make the ice cream, again blend the base with an immersion blender until smooth and creamy.

3 Pour into an ice cream maker and freeze according to the manufacturer's instructions. Once the ice cream is finished freezing, gently fold in the doughnut pieces. Package it by alternating layers of ice cream and pockets of Coffee Caramel Sauce. Take care not to fold or stir, as the swirl will churn into the ice cream. Store in an airtight container and freeze overnight.

4 This ice cream is best served as fresh as possible. The doughnuts, while delicious, will become stale after a day or two.

# GRAPE-NUTS
## ICE CREAM

It's hard to measure the amount of derision I've endured over the years for unabashedly owning my love for Grape-Nuts cereal. I never did understand how severely unhip my crunchy little barley nuggets were, although I can say now that I understand why Post never launched a campaign exalting its ingredients. (Try these Peanut Butter Puffs made with Real Peanut Butter! And also, Grape-Nuts made with Real *Dried Yeast*—grab a spoon, kids!)

In defense of Grape-Nuts, I created an ice cream flavor that pays homage to their malty, nutty goodness. What you have here is a confectionery conflation of my favorite things that is far and away among my top flavors. I've long suffered an internal scuffle over whether I prefer crunchy or soggy Grape-Nuts. Their separation into halves allows some to be a bit softer and others to be crunchier. If you prefer the texture one way or another, feel free to adjust accordingly; this is a Grape-Nuts-judgment-free zone.

### MEET ITS MATCH
**Doughnut Ya Love Coffee Ice Cream** (*page 94*), **Strawberry Pop-Tart Ice Cream** (*page 70*), **Salty Buttered Honey Ice Cream** (*page 80*) with **Quick Pickled Berries** (*page 40*), **Roasted Cherry Chocolate Snap Ice Cream** (*page 86*); **Saturday morning cartoons and stretchy shorts**

Blank Ice Cream Base (page 54)
1/2 cup malted milk powder
1 cup Grape-Nuts cereal, divided

1 Prepare the blank base according to instructions.

2 When you're ready to make the ice cream, again blend the base with an immersion blender until smooth and creamy. Add the malted milk powder and continue blending until completely dissolved.

3 Add half the Grape-Nuts and return to the refrigerator for 30 minutes. Soaking the Grape-Nuts is meant not only to infuse more flavor from the cereal but also to produce 2 different textures in the finished product—crunchy and slightly softened. If you prefer not to include the softened cereal, you can strain the solids at this point.

4 Pour the mixture into an ice cream maker and freeze according to the manufacturer's instructions.

5 Just before the ice cream is finished churning, sprinkle in the remaining Grape-Nuts and allow the beater to distribute them.

6 Store in an airtight container and freeze overnight.

# OATMEAL CINNAMON

MAKES ABOUT 1 QUART  *ICE CREAM*

There's nothing terribly groundbreaking here: two flavors that love each other boundlessly, in breakfast and in health, in cookies and in rolls, for richer or for porridge.

And the by-product makes one killer bowl for breakfast. Or sunrise dessert.

**Blank Ice Cream Base (page 54)**
**1 cup oats**
**1 tablespoon ground cinnamon**

1  Prepare the blank base according to instructions.

2  In a small skillet over medium heat, combine the oats and cinnamon. Toast, stirring regularly, for 10 minutes, or until browned and aromatic.

3  To infuse, add the toasted cinnamon and oats to the base as they come off the stove and allow to steep for about 30 minutes. Using a mesh strainer set over a bowl, strain the solids, pressing through to ensure that you get as much of the flavored cream as possible. A bit of oatmeal pulp may come through, but that's okay—it's delicious! Reserve the oatmeal solids for the oatmeal recipe on page 133!

4  You will lose some mix to absorption, so the yield on this ice cream will be slightly less than usual.

5  Store the mix in your refrigerator overnight. When you're ready to make the ice cream, again blend it with an immersion blender until smooth and creamy.

6  Pour into an ice cream maker and freeze according to the manufacturer's instructions. Store in an airtight container and freeze overnight.

## MEET ITS MATCH
**Savannah Sweet Tea Ice Cream** (*page 165*), **Bananas Ferrari Ice Cream** (*page 62*), **Feta Tomato Swirl Ice Cream** (*page 78*); **Coffee Caramel Sauce** (*page 30*), candied bourbon peanuts, a dollop of apple butter and a hot cup o' joe on an autumn morning

# ICE CREAM SCOOP SELECTION

Proper tools are of utmost importance in any trade. Ice cream scoops over the years have undergone innovations and overhauls. Let's explore the most common options and their freezer-ready features.

## DISHER

With spring-loaded levers and a scraping mechanism designed to oust ice cream before it can feel too at home in the bowl of the scooper, these were all the rage for a while. Unfortunately, their susceptibility to spring-related ruin has left many on the scrap heap.

## SPADE

The spade's association is often with gelato; ordering a cone in its home country of Italy usually results in a visually haphazard, amorphous mass, a towering treat that is unwieldy, unrestricted, and totally unwilling to be tamed. In the United States, spades have become more popular with the introduction of gelato-style shops, but most consumers still can't wrap their heads around the noncircular ice cream service.

## CLASSIC DIPPER

Nothing fancy here, just your standard scooper. Depending on the type of metal, however, ice cream has a tendency to adhere to the bowl of the dipper, refusing to abdicate its residency once comfortably inside.

## HEAT-TRANSFER-HANDLED

Inside the handle of these industry-favored scoopers lives a fluid that harnesses the heat from the operator's hand and transfers it to the bowl of the scoop. This allows the ice cream to easily disengage from the metal.

It is sometimes advised to dunk your dipper in warm water between scoops to loosen and warm the ice cream as you cut through. By doing so, you introduce water droplets to the frozen surface of the ice cream each time you return for a scoop. This means that you're essentially creating icicles on the surface of your 'scream. *¡No bueno!* It's far more prudent in the long run to exercise a little patience and allow the ice cream to come up to a scoopable temperature.

ICE CREAM ROAD MAP

# CHAPTER 3

# SOFTER-SERVE

There's something about soft-serve. The image of an expertly pulled cone, the symmetry of its star-shaped swirls and marshmallowy texture, the blending of chocolate and vanilla into one singular and contiguous stream, the way it clings to the cone when being rolled in a spectacle of toothsome sprinkles or inverted into a warm bath of chocolate dip, its milky, pure appearance—it's total magic.

I love soft-serve so much that when I was married, we dispensed with the standard layer cake and invited Mister Softee to cater our wedding. My favorite photos from that day aren't of a walk down the aisle but, rather, of our parents and grandparents, smiling like 6-year-olds, showing off their chocolate-and-vanilla swirls, their dipped-top cones, and their banana splits; it's transportive, nostalgic.

# AN AT-HOME SPIN ON SOFT-SERVE

PEPPERMINT COCOA COOKIE
SOFTER-SERVE **103**

GRAPEFRUIT-HONEY
SOFTER-SERVE **105**

SWEET CREAM SOFTER-SERVE
**106**

GINGER LEMONADE
SOFTER-SERVE **106**

MEXICAN MUSCOVADO
CARAMEL SOFTER-SERVE **107**

KEY LIME VANILLA BEAN
SOFTER-SERVE **108**

BROWN SUGAR SOUR CREAM
SOFTER-SERVE **108**

ROOT BEER & GOAT CHEESE
SOFTER-SERVE **111**

IMPERIAL ARBORETUM
SOFTER-SERVE **112**

SEA SALT & SOURDOUGH
SOFTER-SERVE **115**

VANILLA, OLIVE OIL &
CACAO NIB SOFTER-SERVE **116**

PIÑA COLADA SOFTER-SERVE **117**

BROWN SUGAR BBQ
SOFTER-SERVE **118**

BITTER CREAMSICLE
SOFTER-SERVE **120**

SALTED ANISE SOFTER-SERVE **121**

LIFE SHOULD BE A BOWL
OF LUXARDO CHERRIES
SOFTER-SERVE **123**

HONEY-LESS NUT CRUNCH
SOFTER-SERVE **124**

# AN AT-HOME SPIN
# ON SOFT-SERVE

YOU'VE READ MY THESIS ON THE SPECIALNESS OF ICE
CREAM. Soft-serve takes that feeling even further. It is even more rare, even
more fleeting—and also so very much more maddening, because I have never
found a successful method for re-creating it at home.

I have spoken with dairy experts and exchanged e-mails with professors and
food science specialists at Ivy League universities. Regardless of the intensive
research, the breadth of techniques and ingredients with which I've
experimented, every outcome and conversation was the same: It's all about the
machine. Commercial machines simply have capabilities with which their
countertop counterparts will never be able to compete.

The following recipes are an answer to this long-developing disappointment.
They aren't exactly soft-serve—in fact, they aren't technically ice cream at all. But
they come fairly close in consistency, and simultaneously, they actually address
another inquiry I get fairly often: Is there a way to make ice cream at home without
an ice cream maker?

The irony and the beauty of this particular formula is that while traditional
soft-serve is so heavily reliant on that piece of equipment, this imitation actually
requires absolutely no equipment at all.

The recipes here rely on the air already whipped into the store-bought topping,
the sweetness in the condensed milk instead of the need to cook and dissolve
sugar, and the introduction of a cream-based product to contribute milk fat and
solids. This product won't freeze quite as cold and solid as the standard base,
which is in part why it mimics soft-serve. The flavors are selected specifically for
this application: The slightly warmer output better serves more delicate flavors
and nuances that might otherwise be camouflaged beneath a more frozen product.
Here they have the opportunity to shine.

By behavior and design, this dessert is similar to a semifreddo, but its
construction—built from store-bought ingredients married in a single bowl—is
a cinch. And for me, its soul is all soft-serve.

# PEPPERMINT COCOA COOKIE

MAKES ABOUT 1½ QUARTS  *SOFTER-SERVE*

It kills my mint-loving soul that so many peppermint chocolate–flavored items are relegated to the month of December. Have we forgotten the grasshopper, people? Please be a responsible snacker and support this flavor year-round.

**12 ounces whipped topping**

**1 can (14 ounces) sweetened condensed milk**

**¾ cup heavy cream**

**2 tablespoons Dutch processed cocoa powder**

**1 teaspoon peppermint extract**

**Seeds scraped from 1 vanilla bean**

**1 cup crushed sandwich cookies (or candy canes for the holidays!)**

In a bowl, gently fold together the whipped topping, milk, cream, cocoa, peppermint, vanilla bean seeds, and cookie crumbs, taking extra care not to deflate the air from the whipped topping. Once well integrated, store in an airtight container and freeze overnight.

## MEET ITS MATCH

**Life Should Be a Bowl of Luxardo Cherries Softer-Serve** (*page 123*), **Marshmallow Whiff** (*page 36*), **Imperial Stout Whip** (*page 47*), **White Chocolate Enchanted Shell** (*page 39*)

**ROCKY ROAD TRIP**

## TENNESSEE

▼ *UTTERLY, NASHVILLE*

Offerings from Utterly, a wholesale-only business, must be sought out for sampling at a certain few establishments where they're served in town. Owner Mayme Gretsch has been trained in world-class kitchens all over the world, from the Michelin-starred Arzak in Spain and Alinea in Chicago to the renowned Catbird Seat in Nashville, but lucky for us she's decided to switch career paths in favor of crafting a line of pastries and ice creams.

Her incredible talents manifest in the form of doughnuts, macaroons, and soft-serve ice cream made with real Tennessee milk. When in Music City, you can treat yourself to her sundaes at Pinewood Social in flavors like Roasted Vanilla or Askinosie Milk Chocolate, topped with seasonal fruit compotes and cookie creations.

**WHAT I'M HAVING:** Whatever's on the menu. I trust Mayme implicitly.

# GRAPEFRUIT-HONEY
## SOFTER-SERVE

MAKES ABOUT 1½ QUARTS

The combination of grapefruit and honey is classic. For breakfast, I like to drizzle honey over the top of a halved grapefruit and brulee the hell out of it. As a cocktail, the Brown Derby—a combination of grapefruit, honey, and bourbon—is outstanding. For lunch, a salad of arugula with grapefruit segments and honey vinaigrette is at once bitter and sweetly satisfying. And at dinnertime, roasted salmon lacquered with honey and grapefruit is unbeatable.

I love a good floral honey here, like white sage, but I've also used darker honeys like buckwheat for more depth of flavor and had a super-satisfying end product. This can easily fill the desire for a more traditional Creamsicle—and a sprinkle of cinnamon on top is killer.

12 ounces whipped topping

1 can (14 ounces) sweetened condensed milk

¾ cup grapefruit juice

4 tablespoons honey

2 tablespoons grapefruit zest

In a bowl, gently fold together the whipped topping, milk, grapefruit juice, honey, and grapefruit zest, taking extra care not to deflate the air from the whipped topping. Once well integrated, store in an airtight container and freeze overnight.

### MEET ITS MATCH

Salted Anise Softer-Serve (page 121), Honey-Less Nut Crunch Softer-Serve (page 124), Sea Salt & Sourdough Softer-Serve (page 115), Hibiscus Whip (page 47), Simple Strawberry Jam (page 43)

# SWEET CREAM SOFTER-SERVE

MAKES ABOUT 1½ QUARTS

A basic, blank canvas recipe, but it is so delicious all on its own. My first instinct is always to serve a scoop with warm apple pie.

**12 ounces whipped topping**

**1 can (14 ounces) sweetened condensed milk**

**¾ cup heavy cream**

In a bowl, gently fold together the whipped topping, milk, and cream, taking extra care not to deflate the air from the whipped topping. Once well integrated, store in an airtight container and freeze overnight.

# GINGER LEMONADE SOFTER-SERVE

MAKES ABOUT 1½ QUARTS

Like a perfect summer day, this is bright and refreshing, with a subtle spicy kick from the ginger.

## MEET ITS MATCH

**Imperial Arboretum Softer-Serve** (page 112)**, Brown Sugar BBQ Softer-Serve** (page 118)**; a gin and tonic and a smile**

**12 ounces whipped topping**

**1 can (14 ounces) sweetened condensed milk**

**¾ cup lemon juice**

**1 tablespoon ground ginger**

**Zest of 1 lemon**

In a bowl, gently fold together the whipped topping, milk, lemon juice, ginger, and lemon zest, taking extra care not to deflate the air from the whipped topping. Once well integrated, store in an airtight container and freeze overnight.

# MEXICAN MUSCOVADO
## CARAMEL SOFTER-SERVE

One of my favorite Christmas gifts in recent memory was from Emily: a sample pack of nine different variations of vanilla bean. Who knew there were so many options? When I was growing up, there was vanilla extract and—well, that was about it. But when you really get geeky about the beans, your plain old vanilla suddenly produces a new personality—maybe with hints of almonds and cherries, or licorice and red wine.

MMC, as it has come to be known, is heavily reliant on Mexican vanilla beans. The tobacco-like qualities of this particular bean combined with the molasses-y muscovado and the process of nearly burning the syrup makes for a deeply complex finished product with notes of smoke, espresso, leather, burnt sugar—it's pure heaven with just a little bit of an edge.

12 ounces whipped topping

14 ounces evaporated milk

¾ cup heavy cream

½ cup Mexican Muscovado Caramel Sauce (page 34)

In a bowl, gently fold together the whipped topping, milk, cream, and Mexican Muscovado Caramel Sauce, taking extra care not to deflate the air from the whipped topping. Once well integrated, store in an airtight container and freeze overnight.

### MEET ITS MATCH
**Peanut butter, dark chocolate, coffee, or Bananas Ferrari Ice Cream** (page 62); a cigar and a walk in the woods

# KEY LIME VANILLA BEAN

**MAKES ABOUT 1½ QUARTS** *SOFTER-SERVE*

Teeny, tiny Key limes. Adorable, wonderful little green orbs of sweet-tart satisfaction. The only real companion they call for is a fragrant vanilla bean—preferably Tahitian—and they simply sparkle.

**12 ounces whipped topping**

**1 can (14 ounces) sweetened condensed milk**

**¾ cup Key lime juice**

**Seeds scraped from 1 vanilla bean**

In a bowl, gently fold together the whipped topping, milk, lime juice, and vanilla bean seeds, taking extra care not to deflate the air from the whipped topping. Once well integrated, store in an airtight container and freeze overnight.

## MEET ITS MATCH

**Hibiscus Whip** *(page 47)*, **Simple Strawberry Jam** *(page 43)*, **Salted Anise Softer-Serve** *(page 121)*, **Mint Cherry Compote** *(page 84)*

# BROWN SUGAR SOUR CREAM

**MAKES ABOUT 1½ QUARTS** *SOFTER-SERVE*

Deeply rich, dark muscovado sugar responds with enthusiasm to the tang and lush texture of sour cream in this base.

**12 ounces whipped topping**

**1 can (14 ounces) sweetened condensed milk**

**6 ounces sour cream**

**4 tablespoons dark muscovado sugar**

In a bowl, gently fold together the whipped topping, milk, sour cream, and sugar, taking extra care not to deflate the air from the whipped topping. Once well integrated, store in an airtight container and freeze overnight.

## MEET ITS MATCH

**So versatile, this flavor can be paired with all manner of fruits, chocolate, caramel, and toppings.**

# ROOT BEER & GOAT CHEESE

MAKES ABOUT 1½ QUARTS *SOFTER-SERVE*

There is a bar in my part-time home of Nashville called Pinewood Social. Well, it's hard to call it a bar, exactly, as it functions more as an adult playground complete with bowling alley, bocce court, swimming pool, and coffee shop. But regardless of what you call it, the food and drinks are some of the most fun in town.

Their steak tartare is out of this world, but one of my favorite offerings is a selection of toasts. Tomato confit and burrata, chicken liver, and other standards are fantastic, but the one that blew me away the first time I ordered it was chèvre and root beer toast.

I'm not sure what brilliant mind realized that these are flavors that belong together, but I commend it. It's like biting into the best root beer float ever made, the slight tang of the goat cheese offsetting the sweet, syrupy soda flavor. If you're so inclined, I say pair this flavor with a spot of Fernet-Branca; the herbal bitter shares some synergies with root beer, and the goat cheese wrangles them together.

**12 ounces whipped topping**

**1 can (14 ounces) sweetened condensed milk**

**6 ounces goat cheese**

**2 tablespoons root beer syrup**

In a bowl, gently fold together the whipped topping, milk, cheese, and root beer syrup, taking extra care not to deflate the air from the whipped topping. Once well integrated, store in an airtight container and freeze overnight.

### MEET ITS MATCH
Serve it like Pinewood on a crusty slice of bread, or top it with Quick Pickled Berries *(page 40)* and be prepared for an explosive flavor profile.

# IMPERIAL ARBORETUM

MAKES ABOUT 1½ QUARTS *SOFTER-SERVE*

During one particularly frustrating navigational flub, I wound up emerging from a trip on the New York City Subway and into a downpour on the wrong side of town. Luckily I could take cover in one of my favorite spots in the city: Chelsea Market. I wound up killing time in the spice market, where I was treated to a sensory analysis of a vast range of teas and blends by some very bored employees grateful for the company during the weather-induced slump.

Though I had no original intention of shopping, I left with a bag full of tins, feeling like I had stepped off a pirate ship from the West Indies. Back at home, I found the Chinese Five-Spice powder and the hibiscus flowers that I picked up to be particularly friendly, so I gave them a frozen place to commune.

**12 ounces whipped topping**

**1 can (12 ounces) evaporated milk**

**¾ cup heavy cream**

**1½ tablespoons five-spice powder**

**2 tablespoons Ginger Hibiscus Syrup (page 27)**

In a bowl, gently fold together the whipped topping, milk, cream, five-spice powder, and hibiscus syrup, taking extra care not to deflate the air from the whipped topping. Once well integrated, store in an airtight container and freeze overnight.

### MEET ITS MATCH
**Chocolate Sorbet** (*page 65*) **and Honeyed Peanut Butter Sauce** (*page 25*) **with Sea-Salted Whip** (*page 45*)

# SEA SALT & SOURDOUGH
### *SOFTER-SERVE*

MAKES ABOUT 1½ QUARTS

Forget Rice-A-Roni—*this* is the San Francisco treat. Sitting bayside in the Golden Gate City, the aromas of sourdough and salt water are perfectly complementary and appropriately emblematic of the city itself. The ice cream is an homage to one of my favorite stateside destinations.

12 ounces whipped topping

1 can (14 ounces) sweetened condensed milk

³/₄ cup heavy cream

2 teaspoons flaked sea salt

¹/₂ cup sourdough bread crumbs

In a bowl, gently fold together the whipped topping, milk, cream, salt, and bread crumbs, taking extra care not to deflate the air from the whipped topping. Once well integrated, store in an airtight container and freeze overnight.

## MEET ITS MATCH
Everything! Chocolate Sorbet *(page 65)*, Root Beer & Goat Cheese Softer-Serve *(page 111)*. Or drizzle with Simple Strawberry Jam *(page 43)* and Honeyed Peanut Butter Sauce *(page 25)* for a spin on breakfast toast.

# VANILLA, OLIVE OIL & CACAO NIB SOFTER-SERVE

MAKES ABOUT 1½ QUARTS

I was once served a single-origin chocolate—just one devastatingly small sample as a part of a larger tasting—that has never vacated my memory. Bitter and viscous, mouth-coating and fruit-forward, the fleeting bite had notes of fragrant vanilla and bright, citrusy olive oil. I melted with it as it evaporated from my tongue, the flavor in bloom while the room fell away.

And while that moment may never truly be recaptured, this flavor is a reimagining based on the memory. I believe that it manages to pull together the most important characteristics —the creamy olive oil, the perfume of vanilla, and the bitter cacao—so that I can almost fool myself into a repeat performance.

**12 ounces whipped topping**

**1 can (14 ounces) sweetened condensed milk**

**½ cup heavy cream**

**2 ounces good-quality extra virgin olive oil**

**Seeds scraped from 1 vanilla bean**

**½ cup cocoa nibs**

In a bowl, gently fold together the whipped topping, milk, cream, oil, vanilla bean seeds, and cocoa nibs, taking extra care not to deflate the air from the whipped topping. Once well integrated, store in an airtight container and freeze overnight.

### MEET ITS MATCH

**Tequila Lime Curd** (page 178) **and Sea-Salted Whip** (page 45)**; a drizzle of Lemon Curd** (page 28)**; your "me" moment**

# PIÑA COLADA
## SOFTER-SERVE

MAKES ABOUT 1½ QUARTS

For Emily's 30th birthday, she had a sole request—that we set up somewhere hot and stay put poolside. I commented, after observing the comically large and elaborately dressed cocktail being delivered to the cabana beside us, that I'd never actually had a piña colada. Em was appropriately appalled at my inexperience with the island-inspired intoxicant and immediately ordered one for us to share.

I'm not sure how the tropical pleasures of the piña colada eluded me until that day, but I'm pretty sure that with the first sip of the over-the-top, umbrella-adorned spectacle of a drink, my eyes turned to cartoon hearts and hula girls began dancing around my head.

I've since done my best to make up for the missed opportunities, and this reinterpretation is now an absolute staple in my summertime entertaining.

**12 ounces whipped topping**

**12 ounces coconut cream**

**¾ cup pineapple juice**

**¼ cup coconut rum**

**2 tablespoons brown sugar**

**Zest of 1 lime**

1 In a bowl, gently fold together the whipped topping, coconut cream, pineapple juice, rum, sugar, and lime zest, taking extra care not to deflate the air from the whipped topping. Additional liquid in this recipe requires a bit more careful mixing, but it will come together.

2 Once well integrated, store in an airtight container and freeze overnight.

### MEET ITS MATCH
**Ginger Lemonade Softer-Serve** (page 106), **a drizzle of Mexican Muscovado Caramel Sauce** (page 34), **and White Chocolate Enchanted Shell** (page 39)

# BROWN SUGAR BBQ

**MAKES ABOUT 1½ QUARTS** — *SOFTER-SERVE*

In downtown Nashville, on the kitschy neon-lighted strip that makes up lower Broadway, most people have their favorite honky-tonks and haunts. For me, that one spot is Rippy's Bar & Grill. There isn't a minute in the day when you won't find killer cover bands, and the Ultimate Nachos piled with pulled pork and plenty of sour cream pair perfectly with the country-music back catalogue.

During one particularly rousing rendition of Garth Brooks's "Callin' Baton Rouge," I realized that the sweet and tangy sauce and the sour cream together could probably be delicious even without all the bells and whistles of pulled pork, jalapeño peppers, and house-made chili. But don't let that stop you from experimenting.

**12 ounces whipped topping**

**1 can (14 ounces) sweetened condensed milk**

**6 ounces sour cream**

**¼ cup muscovado sugar**

**3 tablespoons barbecue sauce**

In a bowl, gently fold together the whipped topping, milk, sour cream, sugar, and barbecue sauce, taking extra care not to deflate the air from the whipped topping. Once well integrated, store in an airtight container and freeze overnight.

### MEET ITS MATCH

**Caramel Ice Cream Braised Pork Shoulder** (*page 152*)**, Better-Than-Buttermilk Biscuits** (*page 132*)**, a drizzle of Tomato Caramel Sauce** (*page 33*)**; Topped with smoked almonds and a drizzle of Bourbon Ganache** (*page 37*)**; the Grand Ole Opry**

# BITTER CREAMSICLE

MAKES ABOUT 1½ QUARTS

## SOFTER-SERVE

Originally inspired by the old-fashioned, a bourbon-based drink that calls for aromatic bitters and is garnished with a shock of orange peel, this flavor wound up telling me what it wanted to be.

Aromatic bitters, particularly the iconic and unmistakable Trinidadian Angostura brand, have a flavor that brags of a baffling, vast (and purportedly secret) array of herbs and spices that prove themselves to be useful in a multitude of classic cocktails. I thought I knew the product's profile well, but once those aromatics were introduced to the cream, its character transformed, falling somewhere between a Creamsicle and an autumn-spiced cider.

12 ounces whipped topping

1 can (14 ounces) sweetened condensed milk

¾ cup heavy cream

15 dashes of aromatic bitters

2 tablespoons orange zest

### MEET ITS MATCH

**Ginger Lemonade Softer-Serve** (page 106), **Mexican Muscovado Caramel Softer-Serve** (page 107), **Imperial Arboretum Softer-Serve** (page 112)

In a bowl, gently fold together the whipped topping, milk, cream, bitters, and orange zest, taking extra care not to deflate the air from the whipped topping. Once well integrated, store in an airtight container and freeze overnight.

**ROCKY ROAD TRIP**

## NEW YORK CITY

### ▼ AMPLE HILLS CREAMERY, MULTIPLE LOCATIONS

The Brooklyn-based operation may be only just a few years old, but it's already a community classic. Owner Brian Smith is one of the great ice cream chefs of the current generation, and his perfectly formulated execution is matched only by his playfulness.

The Munchies gives kids and adults everything they've ever wanted in a dessert—pretzel-infused ice cream with Ritz Crackers, potato chips, pretzels, and M&M's—while more streamlined staples like Sweet as Honey (sweet cream with homemade honeycomb candy) appeal to all ages as well. Everything is homemade, and I have yet to come across an option that doesn't put a smile on my face.

**WHAT I'M HAVING:** Pistachio Squared or their house-made soft-serve in a rotating selection of equally awesome flavors

# SALTED ANISE

MAKES ABOUT 1½ QUARTS

## *SOFTER-SERVE*

had had it. One too many times I'd reached for a blueberry jelly bean only to have the abhorrent, loathsome realization that I had in fact ingested the black licorice variety, too late to save myself the suffering.

But one day while standing in line at Salt & Straw, happily anticipating my ice cream cone, I noticed a package marked "Salty Black Licorice," made by the Jacobsen Salt company. My brand-loyal behavior kicked in: an ice cream shop that I loved, and a product from another company that I knew to be fantastic. I worried that I would live to rue the day, but I bought the damn box.

Later on, after carefully unwrapping a piece of the taffylike, so-blue-it's-black candy as if disarming a bomb, I had my own explosive experience. Holy hell, that thing was *delicious*. It was unlike any item parading itself as licorice that I'd ever tasted before. Here's the un-black version of that salty anise flavor.

12 ounces whipped topping

1 can (14 ounces) sweetened condensed milk

¾ cup heavy cream

2 teaspoons flaked sea salt

1 tablespoon anise extract

In a bowl, gently fold together the whipped topping, milk, cream, salt, and anise extract, taking extra care not to deflate the air from the whipped topping. Once well integrated, store in an airtight container and freeze overnight.

## MEET ITS MATCH
**Mint Cherry Compote** *(page 26)* **or Coffee Caramel Sauce** *(page 30)*, **Ginger Lemonade Softer-Serve** *(page 106)*, **Bitter Creamsicle Softer-Serve** *(opposite)*, **Imperial Arboretum Softer-Serve** *(page 112)*; **incredulity**

— **121** —

# LIFE SHOULD BE A BOWL OF
# LUXARDO CHERRIES

### MAKES ABOUT 1½ QUARTS
## SOFTER-SERVE

Good bars know that a good Manhattan isn't complete without a good cherry. And as far as I'm concerned, the best of all cocktail-accompanying cherries is the Luxardo cherry. Imported from their home in Luxardo, Italy, these cherries bear exactly *zero* resemblance to the Shirley Temple–swimming, unnaturally incandescent, stop-light-red spheres that are a sorry excuse for a stone fruit.

No, these are *exotic*. Each jar makes its transatlantic journey in a comfortable bath of thick, deeply garnet syrup; inherently they're sour, but the sticky preparation results in sweet-tart—and still somehow totally grown-up—lip-smacking satisfaction. I can't tell you what sorcery is employed in their creation. I don't know the enchanted tree that produces these perfectly candied cherries.

I began putting them on and in just about anything—oatmeal in the morning, sandwiches in the afternoon, a show-stopping Luxardo cherry duck sauce (which, let me tell you, is *divine*) once or twice for dinner. But their real sweet spot is in this blending of fruit and cream, and using both the cherries and the syrup here ensures the utmost level of Luxardo-ness.

If I had a nickel for every time I stole a Luxardo cherry off the counter when a bartender wasn't looking, well, I'd buy a whole lot more Manhattans. And then I'd make a whole lot more of this stuff, too.

**12 ounces whipped topping**

**1 can (14 ounces) sweetened condensed milk**

**¾ cup heavy cream**

**¼ cup syrup from Luxardo cherries jar**

**½ cup chopped Luxardo cherries**

**Seeds scraped from 1 vanilla bean**

In a bowl, gently fold together the whipped topping, milk, cream, syrup, cherries, and vanilla bean seeds, taking extra care not to deflate the air from the whipped topping. Once well integrated, store in an airtight container and freeze overnight.

### MEET ITS MATCH
**Serve alongside a scoop of Chocolate Sorbet (page 65); top with Bittered Bourbon Peanuts (page 175) and Imperial Stout Whip (page 47).**

# HONEY-LESS NUT CRUNCH
SOFTER-SERVE

MAKES ABOUT 1½ QUARTS *SOFTER-SERVE*

Bee pollen has long been used by herbalists as a "superfood" with purported health benefits ranging from softening skin to treating eczema to addressing alcoholism (huh?). Simply eating it for enjoyment doesn't seem to have been common practice.

Unlike fennel pollen, which is powdery in consistency, bee pollen presents in much larger granules. They actually look a little like Grape-Nuts (perhaps that's what originally drew me in). The flavor is mild but unique, definitely not to be confused with that of traditional honey. Typically, bee pollen is pleasantly floral, occasionally bitter, and sometimes even a tad nutty. Since the pollen can come from a variety of flowers, both the taste and color can vary. Texturally is where it really brings some buzz; it's kind of like nature's sprinkles.

After revisiting one of my favorite toasted oat cereals, though, I got to thinking about how it'd nicely pair with the toasted almond flavor. I chose to use it in the soft-serve iteration because I love the way the pollen pellets punctuate spoonfuls of the light and creamy base.

**12 ounces whipped topping**

**1 can (14 ounces) sweetened condensed milk**

**¾ cup heavy cream**

**1 tablespoon almond extract**

**½ cup bee pollen**

In a bowl, gently fold together the whipped topping, milk, cream, almond extract, and bee pollen, taking extra care not to deflate the air from the whipped topping. Once well integrated, store in an airtight container and freeze overnight.

### MEET ITS MATCH
**Mexican Muscovado Caramel Sauce** (*page 34*), **Sea-Salted Whip** (*page 45*); **Grapefruit-Honey Softer-Serve** (*page 105*). **Ginger Lemonade Softer-Serve** (*page 106*); **adorable cartoon insects**

# ICE CREAM ENTERTAINMENT

There's more to sharing ice cream than simply scooping a few servings from a store-bought pint container. If you're planning to do a dinner party with a frozen dessert finale, here are some tips to demonstrate ice cream savvy that will dazzle your diners.

## ORDER OF APPEARANCE

At the Hay Rosie Tasting Room, I asked this question often and was surprised at how frequently I was met with expressions of appreciative awe. "Well, *thank you* for asking!" people would gush, as if grateful that I'd finally noticed their new hairdo.

To me, it seemed like a natural question, the response being such a determining factor in the way an ice cream experience will be remembered.

The inquiry that garnered such gratitude from fans was a very simple one: Which flavor would you like on top?

You see, the order of appearance changes everything. There's a method, a process, and an experience to anything that we eat. With ice cream, it's pretty safe to say that those first few bites will be enchanting almost no matter what—maybe because we've been thinking about them all day, or because it was an unexpected and pleasant surprise trip to the ice cream parlor. We're excited, and our palates are primed and ready.

That top flavor, the one we eat first, will still be quite cold and firm from its time in the freezer. When we ingest anything that is too cold or too hot, our taste buds become defensively shy out of self-preservation, dulling the taste of whatever it is that we're striving to savor. With that in mind, the top scoop should be a strong flavor, something assertive enough to grab the tongue's attention.

By the time we've enjoyed that initial scoop and burrowed our way into the bottom flavor, it's become a bit softer and melted, and, at these warmer conditions, it has had the opportunity to open up and bloom, much like wine. More delicate flavors perform better under these circumstances, when the temperature has been allowed to climb slightly and the aroma molecules can volatilize.

Also, if it's a flavor with large or crunchy inclusions—like Maltese Pecan or a chocolate chip cookie dough—the bottom is an ideal position. Fresh from the freezer, these flavors can be difficult to enjoy while the ice cream itself is still particularly firm and the mix-ins too frozen in place to fish out. At that point, they'll also be quite hard and potentially hazardous to the chompers.

Also consider that if the serving vessel is a cup, there's a good chance that a bit of the leading flavor will melt into the supporting scoop, while the former will likely be consumed mostly unadulterated. That factor is critical to building the ever-important final bite.

When serving your guests, if you want to garner the most ice cream gratitude, always give them the benefit of being able to choose the structure of the stack.

## CUP OR CONE

Ah, an age-old conundrum. For me, the answer to this question has always come down to the style of ice cream. Hard scoop I prefer in a cup. Soft-serve, always a cone. I could give you my reasons, but they're of personal preference, and I wouldn't want to unduly influence your decision.

But when it comes to entertaining, you'll have to choose whether you want to offer your guests both options or just one. Cups are clearly the simpler way to go. Just set out a stack and it can be a self-serve situation. You'll also have more flexibility when it comes to toppings and accoutrements.

Cones require a bit more hosting involvement. As an ice cream professional, I don't feel ashamed to tell you that I still struggle with exemplary cone service, particularly in a home setting. The temperature of your freezer, the tools at your disposal, and the types of cones you can access will all impact the outcome of your cone service.

On the flip side, cones can certainly be a bit more festive. There's something about the act of eating one that can't help but be fun. It's one of the few times that, regardless of age, we can be reasonably expected to eat with our hands, to stick out our tongues and tilt our heads and be totally distracted by the dessert before us. It becomes an engaging party activity rather than a passive (though perhaps more distinguished) dessert experience.

## CONE SELECTION

If you opt to offer cones, now you'll have to consider which ones and why. Waffle, wafer, sugar—each classic cone has its own distinctive flavor and texture, and those are factors frequently overlooked. The cone is in and of itself a treat and shouldn't be dismissed as simply a kickstand for your ice cream. To revisit that critical Final Bite, the cone is going to be about 60% of it! You just can't overlook its importance.

To me, the fact that you'll walk away from an ice cream with the flavor of your cone left to linger makes it a pivotal piece. I've actually polled people to find out why they chose the cones that they did. Many said it was out of habit. Others said aroma had a great deal of impact (waffle cones, it is interesting to note, are overwhelmingly confused with the "smell" of ice cream).

And while delicious on its own, the taste of the cone must be acknowledged. Pairing a cone with a cream is just as important as negotiating a Nebbiolo or a Barolo for a beef dish. There are personalities to balance in both. It's time we start to make that determination based on flavor, application, and environment (inside or out? hot summer day or holiday party?).

Let's review what we've got to work with.

**WAFFLE:** A card-carrying member of the World's Most Wonderfully Smelling Products club, this is the kind of cone that

many ice cream shops will venture to make on-site, although commercially made varieties are available at less-ambitious parlors as well as grocery stores for at-home consumption.

These are the softest of the cones. On the plus side, that means that biting into one won't be terribly incongruous with the ice cream eating experience, but on the other hand, the softness of a waffle cone can result in a rapid sog-ifying that can be unpleasant or—worse—structurally unsound. And despite best efforts, handmade versions also tend to inevitably have a slight opening at the bottom, which means that as the ice cream melts, the eater must either expedite the enjoyment process (rushing through ice cream enjoyment is perhaps one of my greatest pet peeves) or plug the bottom with some makeshift stopgap measure.

Typically, waffles are also the largest, offering to support the most ice cream per square inch. While the flavor of a waffle cone can range, honey and brown sugar find their way into most flavor profiles. The process of cooking these cones on a waffle iron also naturally caramelizes their inherent sugars, resulting in a toasty and rich chew.

**SUGAR:** The sturdiest of the ice cream stanchions, sugar cones are thick-walled, crisp, and quite small by comparison to the waffle cone. Bite-ability can be tricky with sugar cones, as they aren't as susceptible to softening by coming into contact with the moisture of the ice cream. If you enjoy your ice cream at a brisk pace, you may reach the cone before it's had a chance to un-brittle. Shattering can be a real risk in that case,

resulting in the need to rush through the remainder of your experience (did I mention I can't stand rushing through ice cream?).

Sugar cones are often made with brown sugar, so again the flavor is a bit more molasses-y, sometimes even grahamlike. While they are damn tasty and so great with lots of ice creams, I'm not a fan of sugar cones with soft serve; the textural difference is just too stark.

**WAFER OR "CAKE":** For some reason, these cones have become associated with "kiddie" sizes and soft-serve-only applications. They've gotten such a bad rap; I've heard them referred to as Styrofoam-like or wet cardboard, and I object to these generalizations.

These cones are made with the least amount of sugar and, thus, are decidedly more neutral. They come in both conical and flat-bottomed breeds, the latter being a nice feature for convenience (making them the singular ice cream cone scenario that can be put on pause).

I do prefer soft-serve with this variety, as those flavors tend to be a bit more delicate; the ice cream itself cannot stand up to the sturdiness of a sugar cone, and it is easily overwhelmed by the assertive caramel and honey notes of a waffle cone.

Structurally, cake cones can be the swiftest to sacrifice their integrity. On a hot summer day, I might not recommend sitting in direct sunlight with one of these. They can become mushy as the ice cream melts, and this results in—you guessed it—the extremely undesirable requirement to rush through your ice cream.

A solid strategy to combat most cone complications is to line the inside of any option with a drizzle of Enchanted Shell and pop it in the fridge or freezer long enough for it to set. This can provide a sweet layer of reinforcement for your cone, but always remember that by employing this tactic, you're introducing another flavor to the Final Bite, so be sure it's a compatible one.

In closing cone arguments, it's safe to say that each has its strengths and each has its holes. Once you've determined your style of ice cream and the flavors you intend to serve, you can more deliberately appoint your pointed scoop supporter.

## SUNDAE BARS

When building a sundae bar, always choose a range of accoutrements and accompaniments. Caramel sauce, hot fudge, and honeyed peanut butter are all delicious—and they're even fantastic together—but you'll need some other types of toppings if you're going to offer an optimal sundae experience. Make sure you have things that crunch, pop, drizzle, and dollop in a range that spans the rich, sweet, tart, and salt-forward staples. Give your guests a safety net by providing something familiar, as well as a reach flavor that's just a little outside their comfort zone.

When catering or consulting for parties and weddings, I suggest a minimum of the following:

✳ **THREE ICE CREAM FLAVORS,** at least one being on the "cleaner" side (less assertive and free of heavy-handed variegates or inclusions) for uncomplicated pairing

✳ **TWO SAUCES,** with one usually being Malted Hot Fudge (page 21), joined by either a fruit-based option like Lemon Curd (page 28) or Simple Strawberry Jam (page 43) or a more decadent selection like Honeyed Peanut Butter Sauce (page 25) or Mexican Muscovado Caramel Sauce (page 34)

✳ **TWO CRUNCHY MIXERS,** such as Bittered Bourbon Peanuts (page 175) and Sea-Salted Chocolate-Covered Pecan Toffee (page 18)

✳ **SPRINKLES.** *Always* sprinkles. They're in a class of their own.

✳ **ONE WHIP** (and if it's only one, I suggest Sea-Salted Whip, page 45)

This configuration ensures that most guests will wind up with the proper combination of textural and flavor variation without becoming overwhelmed by options.

When creating a self-serve sundae station, keep in mind that most folks are just giant children who rarely have a chance to let their sweet flag fly. There can be a tendency to go a little wild when given free rein at an ice cream buffet after wearing adult pants for far too long. It's a good friend and host who offers guidance to guests, making suggestions on sundae construction and complementary flavors, and encourages seconds so people don't feel compelled to eat everything all at once.

But since you can't always impose that strategy on everyone, you'll want to at least create a selection of options that work reasonably well together.

# CHAPTER 4

# OFF THE CONE

This is where things get really twisted.

Have you ever considered using melted ice cream as a replacement for the cream in your oatmeal? Or as the base dairy for a luscious chocolate ganache? Did you know that you can turn it into your own custom ice pop? How about ice cream hot cocoa? This section takes ice cream at its most basic form—an emulsion of sugar, milk, cream, and other additions—and uses that combination as an ingredient all its own.

Many of these can also function as a practical reincarnation of leftover or left-out ice cream. Instead of tossing out perfectly good (and often pricey) pints, let's talk about how to turn melted ice cream into doughnuts, breakfast, or bonbons—and save your tears for something truly sad, like when you've run out of Better-Than-Buttermilk Biscuits. . . .

## ICE CREAM REINCARNATED

## SAVORY & SUPER-DELICIOUS ICE CREAM APPLICATIONS

# BETTER-THAN-BUTTERMILK BISCUITS

MAKES EIGHT 3" BISCUITS

I am fortunate enough to live a portion of the time in the South. And for all the cultural incongruities with my distinctly Yankee upbringing, one thing is impossible to deny—the folks there know how to eat, and nearly everyone has a secret recipe for *something*.

I haven't been let down yet. If they tell me it's delicious, you bet your biscuits it is. And most of the time they're more than happy to share (if not force on you) their homemade what-have-you.

But that willingness to share stops at the jar. Recipes are sacred, and small details are fiercely guarded and hotly contested between families and friends.

With that in mind, I began the risky business of quietly minding my own biscuits. And in a decidedly un-southern move, I'm going to share my secret with you: It's all in the ice cream. My preference is to use a salted caramel or a good vanilla bean. But I've also made these with blueberry ice cream or even peanut butter for a fun spin on the classic.

**2 cups all-purpose flour**

**1 teaspoon salt**

**4 teaspoons baking powder**

**$\frac{1}{2}$ teaspoon baking soda**

**6 tablespoons cold unsalted butter, cubed + $\frac{1}{4}$ cup melted**

**1 cup melted ice cream, flavor of your choice**

**1 tablespoon flaked sea salt**

1 Preheat the oven to 425°F. Line 2 baking sheets with parchment paper.

2 In a large bowl, sift the flour, salt, baking powder, and baking soda together to combine. Add the cubed butter and toss to coat. Cut the butter into the flour until the mixture becomes shaggy.

3 Make a well in the center of the bowl and add the ice cream. Gently combine the ingredients.

4 When the dough is moistened and comes together, turn it onto a lightly floured surface. Press the dough into a 1"-thick square. Lightly flour the surface of the dough.

5 Use a floured biscuit cutter to cut the dough into squares.

6 Transfer the squares to the prepared baking sheets. Refrigerate for 10 to 15 minutes. Brush with the melted butter and top with flaked sea salt.

7 Bake for 12 to 15 minutes until the biscuits are risen and golden brown. Serve warm as an appetizer or as dessert!

## MEET ITS MATCH

**For a perfect ice cream sandwich, serve these biscuits warm with a scoop of your favorite ice cream inside for a flaky, buttery bite.**

# THE ONLY OATMEAL
## YOU'LL EVER NEED

The oatmeal aisle at the grocery store has become a little overpopulated these days. Make this recipe and never again find yourself overwhelmed by the wall of boxed options at your local market.

**1 cup oatmeal steeped in ice cream base (leftover by-product from Oatmeal Cinnamon Ice Cream, page 97)**

**¼ cup milk, or to preference**

**½ cup golden raisins**

**½ cup Bittered Bourbon Peanuts (page 175)**

**1 banana, sliced**

1. Cook the oatmeal in a small saucepan, over low heat, stirring continuously until warm. Add the milk as needed to reach the desired consistency (I prefer a thick oatmeal, but more milk will produce a looser finished product).

2. Remove from the heat and stir in the raisins, peanuts, and banana. Serve warm for breakfast, lunch, dinner, or dessert.

### MEET ITS MATCH
**A cup of coffee and the Sunday paper**

# MELTED ICE CREAM
MAKES 8 TO 12 **PANCAKES**

Once I realized just how basic it was to build pancakes from scratch rather than the store-bought box, I felt as if I'd been lied to my whole life. Sure, just-add-water makes it seem like a cinch, but when you take into account the wildly superior flavor of scratch-made, skillet-fresh hotcakes, there's hardly a reason to go back.

Replacing the milk that's standard in most pancake recipes with a melted ice cream gives you that chance to cleverly flavor the flapjacks in a way that's subtler than simply dumping additional ingredients into the cooking cakes.

Strawberry ice cream makes a killer pink-hued pancake, and you never even have to worry about seeds sticking in your teeth. Bananas Ferrari Ice Cream (page 62) imparts that banana flavor without whole slices of the fruit (which can become slightly slimy when swimming in batter).

The use of melted ice cream also precludes the need for additional sugar in the mix, as you'll be obtaining an adequate amount of sweetness from the flavor of your choice.

1½ cups all-purpose flour

2½ teaspoons baking powder

¾ teaspoon salt

1 large egg

1½ cups melted ice cream, flavor of your choice (my favorite: Oatmeal Cinnamon Ice Cream, page 97)

Seeds scraped from 1 vanilla bean

2 tablespoons melted butter

1 Preheat the oven to 200°F.

2 In a medium bowl, sift together the flour, baking powder, and salt. In a large bowl, whisk together the egg, ice cream, vanilla bean seeds, and butter.

3 Gradually whisk the flour mixture into the egg mixture until well incorporated.

4 Place a large skillet over medium heat and coat it with nonstick cooking spray or butter. Test the heat by sprinkling water on the pan; if it sizzles, it's ready to go.

5 Drop the desired amount of batter into the skillet (I like silver dollars). Once small bubbles form and begin to pop, flip the pancakes. Repeat until all the batter has been used. Keep cooked pancakes warm on a baking sheet in the oven until ready to serve.

# MELTED ICE CREAM
## MAKES 6 SLICES FRENCH TOAST

The only thing that could make French toast more of a dessert is to use dessert as an ingredient. This is a sneaky strategy for adding a flavorful (and distinctly American) twist to your favorite Francophile breakfast dish. The sugars already present in the ice cream caramelize deeply when introduced to a hot skillet.

Top it with ice cream should you feel so inclined, or even make Freedom Toast ice cream sandwiches.

Why? Because 'Merica.

2 eggs

2 cups melted ice cream, flavor of your choice (caramel, peanut butter, and banana are my favorites)

1/2 teaspoon salt

1 teaspoon ground cinnamon (optional)

1/2 tablespoon butter

6 slices thick bread (I love sourdough, but this recipe will also work with challah or other thick-cut breads)

Maple syrup or topping of your choice

Flaked sea salt

1 Preheat the oven to 375°F.

2 In a medium bowl, whisk together the eggs, ice cream, salt, and cinnamon (if using).

3 Melt the butter in a medium skillet over medium heat. Dredge the bread in the egg mixture and sear it in the hot skillet for about 2 minutes, or until golden brown. Flip using a spatula and sear another 2 minutes, or until golden on both sides.

4 Transfer the cooked slices to a shallow baking pan and bake for about 8 minutes.

5 Serve with maple syrup or another topping of your choice and a sprinkle of flaked sea salt.

### MEET ITS MATCH
Mint Cherry Compote (page 26), Maple-Molasses Cranberry Sauce (page 24). Top with Honeyed Peanut Butter Sauce (page 25), Marshmallow Whiff (page 36), and Quick Pickled Berries (page 40).

# INSIDE-OUT
# CARAMELS

MAKES 60

If we can put caramel in ice cream, why not put ice cream in caramel? Soft, chewy caramels are punched up by the substitution of melted ice cream for the standard-issue heavy cream. Try them with peanut butter ice cream, or get really self-referential with salted caramel salted caramels.

1/3 cup corn syrup

1 cup muscovado sugar

1/2 cup organic cane sugar

1 cup melted ice cream

6 tablespoons butter, cut into chunks

1/2 teaspoon ground cinnamon

2 teaspoons flaked sea salt

1 Line a 9" × 9" baking pan with parchment paper. Allow the parchment to hang over the sides, as you'll later use it to lift out the set caramels. Brush with melted butter.

2 In a medium saucepan over medium heat, combine the corn syrup and sugars. Cook until the sugars are completely dissolved and the mixture reaches 320°F on a candy thermometer.

3 Meanwhile, in a separate saucepan over low heat, warm the ice cream slightly.

4 When the sugar mixture registers 320°F, remove from the heat and *carefully* stir in the warm ice cream and butter. Finally, add the cinnamon and salt and stir until well incorporated. Return the pan to medium heat and cook until the mixture reaches 240°F.

5 Remove from the heat and pour over the parchment paper in the baking pan. Use an offset spatula to level the caramel, then allow it to cool completely in the refrigerator. Once fully set, several hours later, use the parchment paper to lift the set caramel from the pan. Cut into 1" squares and sprinkle with additional flaked sea salt.

## SUGGESTED RIFF

These caramels are pretty much perfection by themselves, but they get a boost from some of the other items in this book. After spreading the caramels onto a baking sheet, sprinkle with Bittered Bourbon Peanuts (page 175) and Quick Pickled Berries (page 40). Allow to set for a twist on PB&J soft caramels.

# POPCORN PUDDING SERVES 4

After finishing a batch of Sriracha Popcorn Ice Cream (page 66), I was left with a bowlful of spent popcorn that had been soaked in ice cream base. I grabbed a spoon for a small sample, and the next thing I knew, I was halfway to the bottom. The flavor of the sweet corn sinking in the rich, sweet mix was like an inverted batch of ice cream. The texture was—admittedly—a little soggy, so I decided to give it a quick sauna.

What emerged from the oven was reminiscent of bread pudding but with all the sunny sweet goodness of freshly popped corn. Take your favorite flavor and put a spin on your pudding; caramel is an obvious choice, as is chocolate-"covered" popcorn. Salty Buttered Honey Ice Cream (page 80) makes your movie theater popcorn feel like a slacker.

Toss the soaked corn with almonds or cashews (or both!) for a little texture before transferring to your baking pan, or sprinkle shredded coconut and raisins on top. The proven possibilities are in the puddin'.

## PUDDING
1½ cups melted ice cream
5¼ cups air-popped popcorn
4 large eggs, beaten

## TOPPING
½ cup muscovado sugar
½ stick butter, room temperature and cubed
1 cup chopped nuts of your choice

1. Preheat the oven to 350°F. Brush four ¾-cup ramekins lightly with olive oil.

2. In a small bowl, combine the butter, nuts (if using), and sugar.

3. Mix together melted ice cream and beaten eggs. Pour over popcorn and allow to sit for 10 minutes.

4. Distribute custard and popcorn mixture evenly among ramekins.

5. Allow to cool slightly, then serve a la mode with your choice of ice cream and Quick Pickled Berries (page 40).

# MELTED ICE CREAM
MAKES ABOUT 12 DOUGHNUTS

How have we *not* been doing this for all of human history? These two things are such natural partners, such kindred spirits, that it only seemed fitting to fit them together in some composition. Your choice of ice cream flavors sweetens the batter, and this recipe produces light, downy doughnuts that allow those nuances to gently endure.

Get really crazy and use Doughnut Ya Love Coffee Ice Cream (page 94) as the ice cream base. Or use these doughnuts *in* Doughnut Ya Love Coffee. Now *that* is some next-level chicken-or-the-egg shit.

3¼ cups bread flour
¾ teaspoon salt
½ tablespoon yeast
¾ cup melted ice cream, gently warmed
4 eggs, beaten
¾ cup butter, cut into ¼" slices
2 quarts rice oil, for frying

1   In the bowl of a stand mixer, combine the flour, salt, and yeast using the dough hook attachment. Add the ice cream and eggs and beat for about 3 minutes.

2   Gradually incorporate the butter. Continue beating for about 3 minutes. Once the dough comes together, form it into a ball and wrap with plastic wrap. Let the dough rest for about 3 hours, and then refrigerate it for 12 to 15 hours, or overnight.

3   The next morning, roll the dough to ¼" thickness and, using a doughnut cutter, stamp out doughnuts and transfer them to a baking sheet. (If you don't have a doughnut cutter on hand, you can use the top of a wide water glass for the outside and a narrow shot glass for the inside.)

4   Allow the doughnuts to proof for 2 hours. When you are ready to fry them, clip a candy thermometer to a Dutch oven or deep saucepan. Bring the oil to 250°F and carefully drop the doughnuts in, allowing a comfortable space between them. Fry for 2 minutes on each side, or until golden brown.

5   Place the fried doughnuts on a drying rack.

6   These are excellent tossed in cinnamon sugar, dipped in Bourbon Ganache (page 37), or coated with Doughnut Glaze (opposite).

# DOUGHNUT GLAZE

ENOUGH GLAZE FOR 18 TO 22 DOUGHNUTS

This classic doughnut glaze is a simple affair. And once again, it presents an opportunity for ice cream experimentation. Try this with your favorite flavor and really customize your doughnut creations.

1½ cups confectioners' sugar
3–5 tablespoons melted ice cream of your choice

Place the sugar in a bowl. Slowly add the ice cream, whisking to incorporate. Add ice cream until the glaze is smooth and pourable but still viscous enough to stick to the doughnuts. Allow the doughnuts to cool before applying the glaze.

**ROCKY ROAD TRIP**

## MULTIPLE LOCATIONS

### ⊽ JENI'S SPLENDID ICE CREAMS

Within our current American ice cream renaissance, one company has been leading the charge, pioneering the world of new-wave frozen desserts—it's an Ohio-born company that has redefined what ice cream could be.

Jeni's Splendid Ice Creams and Jeni Britton Bauer herself have been hugely inspirational to me, providing both endless enjoyment and the impetus for absurdly long road trips and late-night freezer raids. While the scoop shops continue to pop up in spots like Los Angeles, Nashville, Charleston, and Atlanta in addition to their Ohio home base, Jeni's by the pint also reaches many grocers' freezer aisles.

There's good reason that this is our new national favorite: The clean and impactful flavors are nothing short of extraordinary.

**WHAT I'M HAVING:** Ndali Estate Vanilla Bean. This preparation, using potently fragrant Ugandan beans, is the gold standard of ice cream's old standby.

# PINT BOTTOM
# BONBONS

If you're like me, you probably don't have any need for this recipe. That's because I typically just eat my ice cream straight from the pint like a perfect animal. But if you're the civilized type who uses a proper scoop to serve ice cream in a bowl, this will certainly come in handy.

Inevitably, thanks to a critical design flaw in the ice cream pint, there are parts of the package that a standard scoop struggles to reach. In those instances, you're left with the "dregs" of the ice cream—usually not quite enough for a full bowl or cone, so those final few bites are left to languish into a melted mess, ultimately met with an untimely trash can introduction. And because it breaks my heart to see any ice cream not fulfill its day-brightening potential, here's what I propose.

**1 recipe Enchanted Shell (page 39)**
**1 pint ice cream of your choice**

1. Line a baking sheet with parchment paper. Then grab a melon baller or a one-half teaspoon and dig right into those corners. Form the ice cream bits into balls, place on the baking sheet, and return to the freezer for 30 minutes to ensure they're fully frozen.

2. In the meantime, prepare the Enchanted Shell (page 39). Remove the ice cream balls from the freezer and, using a toothpick, dredge each one in the shell mixture. Working quickly, return them to the parchment-lined sheet and to the freezer.

3. Once set, these can be stored in an airtight container and kept frozen. That is, unless you inevitably find yourself standing before the freezer every 5 minutes or so, stealing morsels. But then again, you said you were the civilized type.

# MELTED ICE CREAM
## POPS

It's always devastating when you turn your back for just a few minutes too long and go back to find that precious container's sweet creams have turned to slushies. Don't worry—we won't let them go to waste.

In addition to some of the melted ice cream recipes in this book, this application keeps the cream closest to its originally intended state.

**Any amount of melted ice cream of your choice**

1   Simply fill an ice cream pop mold with your melted ice cream and refreeze it. I know what you're thinking: "You said refreezing melted ice cream would make bigger ice crystals." True, I did say that. But here we're not striving for super-creamy and scoopable ice cream. Ice cream pops, as opposed to ice cream itself, are quiescently frozen treats. That means—by way of an unnecessarily big word—that they are frozen without agitation. Since we're not attempting to whip a bunch of air into the product, we're going to wind up with an equally delicious (albeit different) iteration of your frozen treat.

2   If you don't have ice pop molds on hand, you can also fill an ice cube tray with the melted ice cream and use sturdy straws in place of the classic wooden sticks.

# MINI CRACKER
## CREAMIES

nother fun way to custom-create ice cream sandwiches fashioned from melted ice cream.

**1 pint melted ice cream of your choice**
**1 package crackers of your choice**

1 Line a baking pan with parchment paper, making sure that the paper hangs over the sides. Pour melted ice cream into the pan and return it to the freezer. Once firm, use a knife to cut the ice cream into squares, using your selected cracker as a guide.

2 Sandwich the ice cream squares between 2 crackers, using your choice of topping as a glue. Honey works well.

### MEET ITS MATCH

Graham crackers, Marshmallow Whiff (page 36), **Malted Hot Fudge** (page 35), and **Salty Buttered Honey Ice Cream** (page 80) for a s'mores take. Or try saltine crackers, vanilla ice cream, **Lemon Curd** (page 28), and **Simple Strawberry Jam** (page 43).

# ICE CREAM REINCARNATED

*THESE RECIPES WERE INSPIRED* by the need to reinvent certain ice cream flavors in a way that would make them portable. Here, they're reincarnated as sturdier, more travel-friendly or less weather-reliant versions for those looking to transport some Sage Chocolate Chip Ice Cream on a road trip sans dry ice or to make Maltese Pecan Ice Cream part of a moveable feast.

# SAGE CHOCOLATE CHIP

*COOKIES*

Blending the sage and sugar infuses the cookies with the herb in a big and aromatic way. These chewy cookies are a fun spin on the classic chocolate chip and a perfect consistency for ice cream sandwiches.

1¾ cups all-purpose flour

1 teaspoon baking soda

½ teaspoon salt

15–20 leaves sage

½ cup + 2 tablespoons organic cane sugar

1 cup butter, softened

1 cup muscovado sugar

2 egg yolks

2 teaspoons vanilla extract

1½ cups chocolate chunks

1  Preheat the oven to 375°F. Line a baking sheet with parchment paper.

2  In a medium bowl, sift together the flour, baking soda, and salt. Set aside.

3  In a food processor, combine the sage and cane sugar. Pulse for 2 to 3 minutes, or until the sage is completely broken down to create a sage-infused sugar. Set aside 2 tablespoons.

4  In the bowl of a stand mixer, cream together the butter, muscovado sugar, and the nonreserved sage-infused sugar. Add the egg yolks one at a time and continue mixing until incorporated. Add the vanilla.

5  Turn the mixer to low speed and add the reserved flour mixture in several additions. Finally, add the chocolate and return to beating at medium speed.

6  Once the dough is well combined, portion it into balls of about 1 tablespoon each and arrange on the baking sheet. Sprinkle with the reserved sage sugar.

7  Bake for 8 to 10 minutes, or until golden brown.

# MALTESE PECAN
## COOKIES

First of all, it's a malted chocolate chip cookie, so . . . duh. Secondly, it has pieces of that insanely addictive toffee in place of standard chocolate chips. And, perhaps most interestingly, if you really want to get all meta on your ice cream making, you can substitute pieces of this cookie—or the cookie dough—into the recipe for Maltese Pecan Ice Cream (page 57).

2 cups + 3 tablespoons all-purpose flour

1 teaspoon baking soda

1 cup butter, softened

1 cup dark muscovado sugar

2/3 cup malted milk powder

2 tablespoons honey

Seeds scraped from 2 vanilla beans

1 teaspoon salt

12 ounces Sea-Salted Chocolate-Covered Pecan Toffee, chopped

1 Line a baking sheet with parchment paper and preheat the oven to 350°F.

2 In a medium bowl, sift together the flour and baking soda. Set aside.

3 In the bowl of a stand mixer, cream together the butter and sugar. Add the malted milk powder, honey, vanilla bean seeds, and salt and mix until well combined. (If you don't have a stand mixer, a medium bowl and a handheld mixer—or good ol' elbow grease—will work as well.)

4 Set the mixer speed to low and gradually add the reserved flour mixture.

5 Turn the mixer off and fold in the toffee. Using a cookie dropper or a tablespoon, portion out the dough on the baking sheet. Bake for 8 to 10 minutes, or until golden brown at the edges. Allow to cool completely, then store in an airtight container.

# SAVORY & SUPER-DELICIOUS ICE CREAM APPLICATIONS

*I'M GOING TO ASK A LOT OF YOU HERE,* and I'll appreciate your confidence in me—your trust that I've done the legwork, compiled the research, conducted the trials, and endured many (*many*) errors so that you can simply sit back and enjoy.

You may scrunch your nose up and tell me I've lost my mind, but I'm prepared to challenge you. Because—let's talk this out—ice cream is simply the slightly different frozen form of your favorite cream sauce. We love pastas with alfredo and lobster with brandy cream. We eat up bisques by the bowlful, bathe our potatoes in buttery garlic creams, and puree sweet corn into creamy cups of steaming chowder.

The versatility of our hero makes it favorable for applications both sweet and, yes, savory. I love to pull these out during a dinner party to let ice cream really show off its range. Prepare to see minds blown.

# CARAMEL ICE CREAM
SERVES 4 TO 5
## BRAISED PORK SHOULDER

Pork is perhaps America's most preferred food as of late. There are no signs that we'll be experiencing hog-focused fatigue in the near future. Once a simple breakfast side, bacon has now found its way into everything from brownies to cupcakes to baklava; I'm pretty sure that discovering new ways to consume a pig has recently outranked playing catch as our national pastime.

I vowed never to make a bacon ice cream. I didn't feel I had any new punches to land. But I found a loophole through which to enter the ring.

This is a riff on a classic milk-braised preparation. I like to use a salted caramel ice cream because it complements the naturally caramel-like notes that come from slow-cooking the meat. You can get creative with your choice: Chocolate ice cream and the spice cache in this recipe mimic a mole sauce, while a peanut butter flavor and chili powder will beckon Thai food–lovers.

**1 tablespoon ground cinnamon (optional)**

**1 teaspoon ground red pepper**

**Kosher salt and ground black pepper to taste**

**2 pounds pork shoulder**

**2 tablespoons butter**

**3½–4 cups melted ice cream of your choice (about a quart of premium, high-quality ice cream)**

**1 cup whole milk, if needed**

1. In a bowl, combine the cinnamon (if using), red pepper, salt, and black pepper. Rub the pork with the mixture. Allow to rest in the refrigerator for 2 hours.

2. Melt the butter in a heavy skillet over medium heat, then add the pork. Sear it for 4 minutes. Turn and repeat the searing process on all sides until the pork is golden brown all over.

3. Once browned, transfer the pork to a large, heavy-bottomed pan (preferably cast iron) or Dutch oven over medium heat. Add the ice cream and bring to a simmer. Continue to simmer for 1½ to 2 hours, or until the liquid has reduced considerably and begun to curdle— this is normal! Turn the meat every 30 minutes.

4. The internal temperature of the meat should reach 145°F, and the meat should come apart easily with a fork. If the liquid has evaporated and the meat is not quite cooked, warm the milk separately in a small saucepan over low heat and add to the pork as needed.

5. Remove the pork from the pan and allow to rest for 10 minutes before serving. Pull the pork with a fork and serve over biscuits, pancakes, doughnuts, or whatever strikes your fancy!

# MUSHROOM-THYME
## ICE CREAM SAUCE

SERVES 4

On an especially frosty New York winter day, my wife and I were attempting to thaw by way of pasta coated with a rich mushroom cream sauce. I'd spent the afternoon grumbling about the dearth of ice cream delivery services in the wintertime, and while the dinner was delicious, I was still distressed about my dessert-free future. Emily suggested that I should be satisfied—after all, wasn't I essentially eating pasta coated in would-be ice cream?

Her brilliant observation became my eventual obsession. I prepared this sauce the following day, and while I continued to complain about the lack of ice cream in its familiar form, this did seem to be a fair compromise.

1 tablespoon butter

$\frac{1}{4}$ cup chopped shallots

2 cloves garlic, chopped

1 cup sliced mushrooms (preferably porcini or morel)

1 cup melted vanilla ice cream

1 teaspoon chopped fresh thyme

$\frac{1}{2}$ teaspoon salt

$\frac{1}{4}$ teaspoon ground black pepper

$\frac{1}{2}$ teaspoon chopped parsley

1 Melt the butter in a small saucepan over medium heat. Add the shallots and cook for 2 to 3 minutes, or until translucent and aromatic. Add the garlic and mushrooms and cook for 4 to 6 minutes, or until softened. Add the ice cream, thyme, salt, pepper, and parsley and heat until gently simmering, stirring regularly.

2 Remove from the heat and serve over linguini or chicken.

### MEET ITS MATCH
**Farfalle pasta, roasted chicken, or freshly made gnocchi**

# HONEY-APPLE-PARSNIP

SERVES 4 *BISQUE*

For many of us, perhaps our primary attempt at executing culinary excellence was making that highly technical and discipline-demanding delicacy commonly referred to as ice cream soup. This dish required that its chef spend a protracted period of time sitting on the playground, possibly in direct sunlight, allowing his or her allocated ice cream cup to morph back into its original liquid state.

Some of us were satisfied with this result in its purest form, while others saw an opportunity. Resourceful recess chefs paired their soup with candies, gumballs, brownies, or leftover bits of lunch. It was the original unfrozen blank canvas.

This recipe is my adult answer to ice cream soup. Thanks to the honey and apples, there is a familiar sweetness while still stepping out into savory territory. Appreciating the parsnip may require a slightly more mature palate than is typical of the recess crowd, though this recipe shamelessly repurposes their technique. This bisque is full-bodied and bone-warming, ideal for cool and crisp autumn evenings.

1 tablespoon butter

2 tablespoons chopped shallots

1 clove garlic, chopped

2 cups cubed parsnips

1 red apple, peeled and cubed

$\frac{1}{2}$ cup vegetable broth

$\frac{1}{4}$ cup apple cider

1 tablespoon honey

1 cup water

1 cup melted ice cream

Olive oil, for drizzling

Candied peanuts, for garnish

1  Melt the butter in a medium saucepan over low heat. Add the shallots and cook for 2 to 3 minutes, or until translucent and aromatic. Add the garlic, parsnips, and apple and cook for 8 to 10 minutes, or until tender.

2  Add the broth, cider, honey, and water and simmer for 10 minutes. Once reduced, add the ice cream and puree using an immersion blender. Serve with a drizzle of olive oil and candied peanuts.

# CHAPTER 5

# ON THE SAUCE AND IN THE COLD

Believe it or not, ice cream loves booze. But how could you possibly know that? It's so often sent to the kiddie table, banished to socialize only with soda pop and cheese curls, enviably eyeing the adults and their beers from beneath the onslaught of oversugared and undersupervised children. Don't these people know it's *decades* past the legal drinking age?

This section is designed to rescue poor old ice cream from its dry destiny. To give it a chance to chase chocolate with whiskey or to try tequila with one of its many complementary coconut flavors. Consider this section ice cream's first semester at college, totally liberated, experimenting with behaviors long deemed inappropriate.

# USING ALCOHOL IN ICE CREAM

AS MUCH AS THE FLAVORS OF ALCOHOL often complement an ice cream, even our hero has to observe the concept of moderation. The trickiest part with booze-infused flavors is that ever-irksome moisture content. When adding a spirit, you've got to calculate and compensate for increased liquid content.

The fact that alcohol doesn't actually freeze also needs to be factored in. Like you and me (probably mostly me), with too much booze, ice cream can get sloppy; if you're not careful, you'll have a pathetic puddle on your hands, a soupy, semi-frozen mess that you wind up having to escort home, help out of its shoes, and put to bed.

On the other hand, alcohol is sometimes churned into an ice cream base with the intention of softening it. If you're finding your scoops too solid, a tablespoon or two of vodka or another neutral spirit will soften the stuff right up.

But if you're going strictly for flavor, bitters are a great way to bring cocktail inspiration to a frozen treat without messing with the formula. So potent are these typically botanical-based ingredients that cocktail recipes often call for just a few dashes. Being that you get significantly more bang for your bitters, a little goes a long way in ice cream creation, too.

Liqueurs and cordials also work well, as they're concentrated and more viscous than a straight-up spirit. They're considerably easier to incorporate into an ice cream because they tend to be syrupy and quite a bit lower in alcohol—often weighing in around 15% to 30%.

Many liqueurs can be incredibly sweet, however—important to note when determining the amount you want to use. Adjusting some sugar out of the base recipe to accommodate can be an important modification under these circumstances.

# FERNET & COFFEE CARAMEL
MAKES ABOUT 1 QUART *ICE CREAM*

Despite a notoriously polarizing flavor profile, the classic Italian amaro, Fernet-Branca, is a personal favorite post-dinner ritual. Occasionally, though, I find myself conflicted over whether I prefer a spot of espresso or the digestivo. So rather than make a choice, I began ordering both. Sometimes I enjoy them side by side, and other times I simply combine them. Being that they're both after-dinner items, it seemed only logical to turn them into dessert.

**Blank Ice Cream Base (page 54)**
**½ cup Fernet-Branca**
**Coffee Caramel Sauce (page 30)**

1  Prepare the blank base according to instructions.

2  When you're ready to make the ice cream, again blend the base with an immersion blender until smooth and creamy. Add the Fernet and continue blending until completely integrated.

3  Once the ice cream is finished freezing, package it by alternating layers of ice cream and pockets of Coffee Caramel Sauce. Store in an airtight container and freeze overnight.

**MEET ITS MATCH**
**Salty Buttered Honey Ice Cream** *(page 80)*, **Peychaud's Bitters Whip** *(page 45)*; a nightcap conversation with friends

# IPI: INDIA PALE

MAKES ABOUT 1 QUART _ICE CREAM_

eer, beer, everywhere but not a drop in this ice cream. Instead, I utilize the ingredients in a Belgian India Pale Ale—malt, Belgian candi syrup, and loads of hops—to get a flavor reminiscent of the beer without the added liquid.

The Bruery's line of Belgian-style ales easily includes some of my favorite brews of all time: sour beers that rival the offerings from their country of inspiration, stouts that surpass 20% alcohol but are as smooth as silk, and wildly creative takes on everything from Thai food to cocktails.

But at the end of a long shift serving and sampling those styles, which are often high in alcohol and on the sweeter side, one thing I constantly craved was a quaffable, hoppy, West Coast IPA to reset my palate. This ice cream pays homage to that hankering.

In order to achieve the intense IPA flavor that I really wanted, I decided that using the beer alone wouldn't get the job done. It could be reduced into a syrup, but with hops, that process could produce a ruthlessly bitter result. Instead, I thought about how the beer is brewed—the infusion of hops into the wort—not unlike an infusion of cream.

So IPI, or India Pale Ice Cream, is made with that process in mind. Replacing the sugar in the base with Belgian candi syrup brings another layer of genuine beer flavor

to the ice cream, while the hops add balance and provide that palate-adjusting punch we Hopheads beg for.

1 ounce hop flowers

1¾ cups heavy cream

5 teaspoons cornstarch

1¾ cups whole milk, divided

½ cup Belgian candi syrup

5 tablespoons nonfat dry milk

½ teaspoon salt

1   In a small saucepan over medium heat, add the hop flowers to the cream. Bring to a gentle simmer for 5 to 7 minutes. Remove the hops and cool the cream completely. Use the infused cream to prepare the base mix according to the following instructions.

2   In a small bowl, combine the starch with 3 tablespoons of the whole milk and whisk until smooth. Set aside.

3   In a nonreactive medium saucepan over medium heat, combine the infused cream, candi syrup, nonfat dry milk, and salt. Whisk until well incorporated. Add the remaining whole milk and cook, whisking frequently.

_(RECIPE CONTINUES)_

4. In the meantime, prepare an ice bath in which to transfer your finished product by filling a large glass bowl with ice.

5. Once the base reaches a boil, reduce the heat and simmer for 4 to 5 minutes.

6. Add the reserved starch-and-milk mixture and cook for 1 minute, stirring constantly with a rubber spatula. Remove from the heat and pour into a storage vessel set over the ice bath. (I typically use a glass Pyrex bowl with a cover, as the base will need to be stored after cooking.)

7. Using an immersion blender, blend the mix well while still warm. This process homogenizes the base and promotes a smoother, creamier finished product.

8. Store the mix in the refrigerator overnight. When you're ready to make the ice cream, remove from the refrigerator and again blend it with an immersion blender until smooth and creamy.

9. Pour into an ice cream maker and freeze according to the manufacturer's instructions.

## MEET ITS MATCH

**Lemon Bar Ice Cream** (page 61), **Imperial Arboretum Softer-Serve** (page 112), **Tequila Lime Curd** (page 178), **Oatmeal Cinnamon Ice Cream** (page 97)

# BASIL JULEP

MAKES ABOUT 1 QUART *ICE CREAM*

By this point you probably assume I'm harboring some deep-seated anti-mint mentality, when in fact it's among my favorites of the herbs. But thanks to an overabundance of basil in my home garden during a brunch party, there were basil juleps all around. The ice cream was simply a natural chaser. If you're mad at me, you can totally use mint instead.

½ cup packed fresh basil
Blank Ice Cream Base (page 54)
½ cup bourbon

1 Gently bruise the basil leaves. In a small saucepan over medium heat, add them to the 1¾ cups of heavy cream used to make the blank base. Bring to a gentle simmer for 5 to 7 minutes. Remove the basil and cool the cream completely.

2 Use the infused cream to prepare the blank base according to the standard instructions.

3 Store the mix in the refrigerator overnight. When you're ready to make the ice cream, add the bourbon and blend with an immersion blender until smooth and creamy.

4 Pour into an ice cream maker and freeze according to the manufacturer's instructions. Once the ice cream is finished freezing, store in an airtight container and freeze overnight.

### MEET ITS MATCH
Savannah Sweet Tea Ice Cream (*page 165*), Peychaud's Bitters Whip (*page 45*), Simple Strawberry Jam (*page 43*), and a drizzle of balsamic vinegar

# SAVANNAH SWEET TEA
**MAKES ABOUT 1 QUART** *ICE CREAM*

Growing up, I was a super-picky kid. My personal Food Pyramid consisted of a slim canon in each category: protein (chicken nuggets), grains (breakfast cereal), fruit (snacks), and vegetables (tomato sauce), among (very few) other things.

In fact, it wasn't until I was 27 years old that I first tasted a peach. It was a gift from a Nashville family, from a local purveyor called the Peach Truck. It changed my world.

The only thing that improves a peach, in my opinion, is another southern specialty: bourbon. This flavor puts them together with a sweet tea base as a tribute to all things southern, with the humble, perfect drupe as its centerpiece.

**2 black tea bags**
**Blank Ice Cream Base (page 54)**
**Bourbon Peach Mint Jam (page 174)**

1  In a small saucepan over medium heat, combine the tea bags and the 1¾ cups heavy cream used to make the blank base. Bring to a gentle simmer for 5 to 7 minutes. Remove the tea bags and cool the cream completely.

2  Use the infused cream to prepare the blank base according to the standard instructions.

3  Store the base in the refrigerator overnight. When you're ready to make the ice cream, add the bourbon and blend with an immersion blender until smooth and creamy.

4  Once the ice cream is finished freezing, package it by alternating layers of ice cream with pockets of jam. Store in an airtight container and freeze overnight.

# TIKI TUESDAY
*ICE CREAM*

Tiki drinks have this party-in-a-(crazy)-glass feeling that is just plain fun. I'd drink them for the serving vessel even if they weren't so scary good, but it just so happens that the hallmarks of this style—the spice blends, the almond-based orgeat, the fruit-forward flavors—make these cocktails prime candidates for dessert reincarnations.

Blank Ice Cream Base (page 54)

3 tablespoons orgeat syrup

2 tablespoons Velvet Falernum liqueur

1 tablespoon Ginger Hibiscus Syrup
(page 27)

### MEET ITS MATCH
Oatmeal Cinnamon Ice Cream *(page 97)*,
Bananas Ferrari Ice Cream *(page 62)*;
summer parties by the bonfire

1. Prepare the blank base according to instructions.

2. Store the base in the refrigerator overnight. When you're ready to make the ice cream, add the orgeat, Velvet Falernum, and Ginger Hibiscus Syrup and again blend with an immersion blender until smooth and creamy.

3. Pour into an ice cream maker and freeze according to the manufacturer's instructions. Once the ice cream is finished freezing, store in an airtight container and freeze overnight.

# COCKTAIL EXPERIMENTS FOR THE ADVENTUROUS ICE CREAM- LOVING BOOZER

*THE SAME DRIVING PRINCIPLES* apply here—a focus on the simple, the fresh, and serious impact. Instead of using ice cream itself as an ingredient, these drinks are designed to incorporate an ingredient *from* an ice cream.

I worked closely with some mix-master friends who helped me understand that, as with a strong ice cream formula, balance is critical to a good cocktail. There's always room to get creative, but try any of these to start out and settle in for a comfortable evening (or afternoon—no one's judging). Each recipe makes one cocktail.

# CURDS AWAY

1 COCKTAIL

Fresh lemon curd brightens up this brown spirit–based drink, making a surprisingly refreshing, citrus-forward staple for summer nights.

2 ounces bourbon

1 ounce lemon juice

3 dashes of aromatic bitters

1 teaspoon Lemon Curd (page 28), or use store-bought

1/2 ounce simple syrup

Fresh or dried blueberries

In a cocktail shaker with ice, combine the bourbon, lemon juice, bitters, Lemon Curd, and simple syrup. Shake vigorously, strain into a coupe glass, and serve up. Garnish with the blueberries.

**ROCKY ROAD TRIP**

## RHODE ISLAND

LICKETY SPLITS, WYOMING

Summertime drives to Newport, Rhode Island, were not worth making without a stop at this roadside stand. The soft-serve is exemplary, and the spot is situated about an hour outside our destination city, which means on the way in it's an anticipation-building pit stop, and on the trip home it serves to soften the return-to-reality blow.

**WHAT I'M HAVING:** Vanilla Soft-Serve with Chocolate Dip

# GIN & JAM

Juice is great and all, but the viscosity of the jam makes for a full and fabulous mouthfeel in this simple cocktail.

¾ ounce lemon juice

¾ ounce simple syrup

2 ounces gin

1 teaspoon Simple Strawberry Jam (page 43)

Fresh mint leaves (optional)

In a cocktail shaker with ice, combine the lemon juice, simple syrup, gin, and jam. Shake briskly to fully dissolve the jam. Strain into a rocks glass over a fresh ice cube and garnish with fresh mint (or sage, or tarragon, or basil) if desired.

# BIG KID PB&J

Let's face it, peanut butter and jelly never gets old, even when we do. The by-product of making Bourbon-Soaked Peanuts is a fantastic Peanut-Washed Bourbon. Hibiscus may be a bit more exotic than classic grape, but its tang mimics the best characters of traditional jelly.

2 ounces Peanut-Washed Bourbon (page 177)

½ ounce Ginger Hibiscus Syrup (page 27)

½ ounce honey

3 dashes of Angostura bitters

In a cocktail shaker or mixing glass with ice, combine the Peanut-Washed Bourbon, Ginger Hibiscus Syrup, honey, and bitters. Stir until thoroughly chilled, then strain into a coupe or martini glass.

# INTOXICATED TOPPINGS, TREATS & SUNDAES

A LITTLE BOOZE CAN GO A LONG WAY in pushing things over the top, and these ideas are just a few to get the party started. Play with different spirits, flavor profiles, and favorite cocktails. Don't be surprised to see an overall spike in satisfaction.

# GINGER TOM COLLINS
## WHOOPIE PIES

MAKES 8

The first time I ever tasted a Tom Collins was in First Tennessee Park, home to Nashville's Minor League Baseball team, which also happens to have a world-class cocktail team behind the Bandbox, the in-park bar. While they can't quite mix you up a Manhattan during the seventh-inning stretch, their selection of simple drinks is better than traditional ballpark boozing options.

I went on an experimental binge exploring the classic cocktail; these whoopie pies with a little ginger were my favorite rendition.

### PIES
1/2 cup butter
1/2 cup muscovado sugar
1 teaspoon baking powder
1/2 teaspoon baking soda
3/4 teaspoon salt
1 egg
1 teaspoon ginger extract
1 1/2 cups flour
1 cup melted ice cream (see note, opposite)
Zest of 1 lemon
Flaked sea salt to taste

### GIN BUTTERCREAM FILLING
1 cup butter
3 1/2 cups confectioners' sugar
1/3 cup gin
1/4 cup heavy cream

1. **To make the pies:** Preheat the oven to 350°F. Line a baking sheet with parchment paper. In the bowl of a stand mixer, using the paddle attachment, beat together the butter, sugar, baking powder, baking soda, and salt until smooth.

2. Add the egg and ginger extract. Reduce the mixer speed and gradually add the flour, then the ice cream. Mix until the batter is smooth and free of any clumps. Fold in the lemon zest.

3. Using a tablespoon or cookie dropper, place dollops of the batter on the baking sheet, leaving about a 2" space between them. These will definitely spread. Sprinkle some flaked sea salt onto each for crunch and pop.

4. Bake for 8 to 12 minutes, or until the cakes puff and a toothpick inserted into one comes out clean. Slide the paper off the pan onto the baking rack and allow to cool completely.

5. **To make the filling:** In the bowl of a stand mixer, beat the butter and sugar until creamy. Add the gin and cream and whip for 4 to 5 minutes, or until fluffy.

6. **To assemble the pies:** Use a pastry bag to pipe filling onto half of the cooled pies. Fit the bottom halves with top halves, using the buttercream to adhere the cakes together.

**NOTE:** It's best to use a neutral flavor here that won't clash with the spice profile. Your classic vanilla works well, or try my favorite from this book—Mexican Muscovado Caramel Softer-Serve (page 107).

# BOURBON PEACH
MAKES 2¼ CUPS *MINT JAM*

oosely based on a peach-infused mint julep, this jam is perfect in ice cream (see the recipe for Savannah Sweet Tea Ice Cream, page 165), on toast, or even served over grilled meats like pork tenderloin.

2 pounds peaches, peeled, pitted, and sliced
2¼ cups organic cane sugar
1⅔ cups muscovado sugar
1½ tablespoons lemon juice
10 leaves mint
2 tablespoons bourbon

1 Store a teaspoon in the refrigerator.

2 In a food processor, pulse the peaches until smooth. Transfer to a large saucepan over medium heat and add the sugars, lemon juice, mint, and bourbon.

3 Bring to a boil, stirring regularly to avoid burning the jam on the bottom of the pan. Continue to simmer for 10 to 12 minutes, or until the jam is thickened. You can test for doneness by dipping the refrigerated spoon into the jam; it should be thick enough that swiping a finger through the jam leaves a clean line.

4 Remove the mint. Allow the jam to cool completely and store in the refrigerator in an airtight container.

5 Leftover jam is delicious on toast or stirred into yogurt or oatmeal.

# BITTERED BOURBON

MAKES 3¾ CUPS *PEANUTS*

Being married to a comedian means getting comfortable with road trips and rest stops. We've driven just about all over the country in our well-worn and road-weary Mazda, and we're intimately acquainted with the country's main arteries, respective gas stations, and motels.

On one such trip through Virginia, we took a gas break, and I informed Emily that I planned to run in for a quick snack. Imagine her surprise when she walked through the entrance after filling up and found me standing in line with a giant sack and a matching smile.

In my search for something to eat, I'd happened upon a selection of local Virginia peanuts. They smelled too damn good to pass up, so I bypassed the 6-ounce snack bag in favor of the 6-pound sack. I sounded like the Bubba Gump of the peanut farm for the remainder of our road trip: "I'm going to make peanut butter, peanut oil, peanut sauce, candied peanuts, roasted peanuts, peanut brittle. . . . "

I still had some of those peanuts a few weeks later when my friend Jarred, cocktail mixer extraordinaire at the Playground in Santa Ana, California, showed me a technique for "washing" bourbon with peanuts. While it produces an incredible infused spirit (which I highly recommend), I was just as interested in the by-product:

bourbon-soaked peanuts. The sweet, salty, spicy, and super-crunchy peanuts are insanely addictive all on their own.

This recipe made me wish I'd gotten a bigger sack. . . .

2 cups Bourbon-Soaked Peanuts (page 177)*

½ cup muscovado sugar

½ cup organic cane sugar

¼ cup water

10 dashes of aromatic bitters (Angostura or the like)

1 teaspoon sea salt

1. Line a baking sheet with a Silpat baking mat or parchment paper.

2. In a medium nonreactive saucepan over medium heat, cook the peanuts, sugars, and water, stirring frequently. Add the bitters and continue to stir until the nuts are toasted and coated in syrup.

3. Remove from the heat and spread in 1 layer on the baking sheet. Sprinkle with the sea salt.

4. Once cooled, break up any clumps, store in an airtight container, and snack aggressively.

*Make sure peanuts have dried entirely before executing.*

# PEANUT-WASHED BOURBON

MAKES 2 CUPS *+ BOURBON-SOAKED PEANUTS*

This super-easy process yields two products that each pack a serious punch: the bourbon-drenched peanuts and a peanut-infused bourbon. This spirit makes a killer cocktail or sipper, but you can also use it as a substitute in Bourbon Ganache (page 37) for a boozy, chocolaty, peanut-buttery snack that could just about bring peace on Earth.

**2 cups unsalted peanuts (if you don't happen upon a roadside sack, simply use your store brand)**

**3 cups good bourbon**

Preheat the oven to 350°F. Spread the peanuts on a baking sheet and toast for about 5 minutes, or until fragrant. Combine with the bourbon in an airtight container and allow to steep for at least 4 days. Strain through a double layer of cheesecloth, and then freeze the liquid for 24 hours. This allows any fat absorbed into the spirit to freeze. Remove from the freezer and strain a second time to separate any fat solids.

**ROCKY ROAD TRIP**

## OREGON & LOS ANGELES

▼ *SALT + STRAW, MULTIPLE LOCATIONS*

By the time I finally had a chance to try Salt & Straw, I had been hearing about them for ages; the bar had reached Olympic-level heights. I waited in the hour-long line at their flagship shop in Portland, and I would easily have gotten right back in line for seconds if my wife would have agreed.

Creative and crazy but, most importantly, well crafted, Salt & Straw's ice creams are brilliant and totally worth the wait.

**WHAT I'M HAVING:** In addition to their standard lineup, they rotate five flavors monthly, specific to each location. The specials are great, but if I'm going with their classic selections, it's Almond Brittle with Salted Ganache, plus Arbequina Olive Oil. S&S has also produced the best nondairy ice cream I've ever tasted— Coconut with Aunt Petunia's Salted Caramel Bars.

# TEQUILA LIME *CURD*  MAKES ¾ CUP

Because frozen margaritas don't always need to be drinkable.

3 egg yolks

½ cup organic cane sugar

¼ cup lime juice

3 tablespoons silver tequila

Zest of 1 lime

4 tablespoons butter, cubed

### MEET ITS MATCH

**Layer on top of fresh strawberries and top with Sea-Salted Whip** (page 45) **for a liquored-up parfait.**

1  Fill a saucepan with about an inch of water and bring it to a simmer over medium-high heat.

2  In a small heatproof bowl, whisk the egg yolks and sugar until smooth. (Reserve the egg whites and make I Pavlova Ice Cream Cake, page 198!) Add the lime juice, tequila, and lime zest and continue to whisk.

3  Set the bowl over the pan of simmering water, being careful that the bowl does not touch the water. Continue to whisk regularly for 8 to 10 minutes, or until the curd has thickened, about to the consistency of a pudding.

4  Remove from the heat and, working in batches, stir in the butter until completely melted and well integrated.

5  Allow to cool completely and store in an airtight container.

# WINTERIZED: ICE CREAM RECIPES FOR COLD-WEATHER ENJOYMENT

*FOR THE LOVE OF ALL THINGS FROZEN*, if I hear one more person tell me in December that it's too cold for ice cream, I'm going to blow a gasket. Honestly, it's not as if I'm asking you to eat it in an igloo. So I'm mounting a full-scale campaign to stop the discrimination—equal rights for ice cream in *all* seasons.

But if you can't quite commit to a cone in its purest condition, try one of these warmed-up options and stop depriving yourself of off-season scoops.

# *THE* HOT CHOCOLATE SHAKE

SERVES 2

During a particularly brutal Brooklyn cold spell one winter, I found myself preparing a couple of piping hot mugs of cocoa in an attempt to stave off the unshakable chill that comes standard with temperatures in the teens.

I was famously frustrated by the body of homemade hot cocoa. It was never as creamy and luxurious as when I purchased a hot cup from a coffee shop. As I stood wrapped in a blanket, mesmerized by the milk swirling on the brink of a simmer, it struck me that it could easily be richer with the addition of melted ice cream.

I incorporated some nonfat dry milk malt, plus starch to take it a step further, and after serving this version, I never complained about homemade hot cocoa again.

Customize at will: Change the ice cream flavor, use dark or milk or white chocolate (or leave it out altogether). Spices or oils or extracts can punch up the flavor, and a little bit of booze never hurts when it's cold out, either.

1 tablespoon nonfat dry milk

1 teaspoon malted milk powder

¼ teaspoon salt

1 teaspoon cornstarch

½ cup melted ice cream

¾ cup whole milk

4 ounces chocolate, chopped

Whipped cream (optional)

1 In a small saucepan over medium heat, whisk together the nonfat dry milk, malted milk powder, salt, cornstarch, ice cream, and whole milk.

2 Heat until simmering, then add the chocolate. Continue to blend until the chocolate has melted. Serve hot, with whipped cream, if desired.

3 Serve in your favorite mug to your absolute favorite person.

## SUGGESTED RIFFS

**CHRISTMAS MORNING HOT SHAKE:** Use peppermint stick ice cream, or vanilla ice cream with 1 teaspoon peppermint oil. Serve with a candy cane garnish, whipped cream, and red and green sprinkles.

**HOT SALTED CARAMEL SHAKE:** Substitute Mexican Muscovado Caramel Softer-Serve (page 34) and top with whipped cream, a drizzle of the MMC Sauce (page 34), and a sprinkle of flaked sea salt.

**HONEY WHISKEY PEANUT BUTTER HOT SHAKE:** Substitute peanut butter ice cream and add 1 teaspoon of your favorite whiskey and 1 teaspoon of a good honey to your saucepan. Drizzle with Bourbon Ganache (page 37) and Honeyed Peanut Butter Sauce (page 25) and top with Sea-Salted Whip (page 45).

# THE CHOCOLATE CHIP COOKIE DOUGH BARNBURNER

**A BARNBURNER HAIKU (OR TWO)**

Toasty Barnburner,
Your cold soul warms mine.
Together, we melt.
Cookie dough blanket
Cover your cool, creamy heart.
Barnburner, my love.

I have often referred to this item as an ice cream sandwich made of dreams because I honestly didn't know how else to describe it. The Barnburner has been a runaway hit and easily the top-selling item at the Hay Rosie Tasting Room. The reason is pretty clear once you've taken a bite: It is like four desserts in one.

Let me try to describe why this crazy confection draws queues of curious ice creamers.

**1. CONTRAST FACTOR:** This is the key to all Barnburners. The contrast of the hot, toasty shell with its slightly crisp exterior against the cold, creamy, and smooth ice cream inside is totally irresistible.

**2. COMFORT FACTOR:** This is the dessert you were never allowed to have. It's basically a chewy, cooked chocolate chip cookie on the very outside, followed by a layer of uncooked dough hiding beneath, and in its belly hides your favorite ice cream flavor—plus any crunchy mix-ins or sauces your heart may desire.

**3. MELT FACTOR:** Ice cream is at its very best taste and texture when it is *just* a little bit melty. The warmer temps allow for optimum mouthfeel and encourage the flavor to truly bloom.

**4. X FACTOR:** I mean, come on. Have you seen this thing?

Commercially, we used a specially designed press to create perfectly formed Barnburners, but at home you can re-create a similar product with a hot skillet and a little finesse.

While there have been many Barnburners concocted (some with greater success than others—I see you, Brownie Batter Barnburner), the Chocolate Chip Cookie Dough is far and away the most popular. For anyone who has ever cleaned the bowl of cookie dough before baking even a single scoop, this one is for you.

Since only the very crust is cooked, the dough is made eggless so you don't have to worry about salmonella when you're on an inevitable Barnburner binge. Chow on, friends.

*(RECIPE CONTINUES)*

1 cup butter, softened

1 cup organic cane sugar

1 cup muscovado sugar

1 teaspoon salt

1 teaspoon vanilla extract

3½–4 cups all-purpose flour

¼ cup vegetable oil

¼ cup heavy cream

12 ounces chocolate chips

Ice cream, flavor of your choice
(1 scoop per sandwich)

1  In a stand mixer, cream together the butter and sugars until light and fluffy. Add the salt and vanilla and continue to mix. Add the flour gradually, 1 cup at a time, with the mixer speed on low. At this point, the mixture will have become quite dry. Add the oil and cream and mix until the dough comes together. Finally, add the chocolate chips.

2  Scoop the dough into balls about the size of a plum, then form each ball into a round patty about the size of a burger. At the Tasting Room, we use ¼ pound of cookie dough per side (that's right, those suckers are full ½-pounders!). At home, you can certainly make them smaller—or larger if your appetite calls for it. Just make sure all pieces are the same size. Use parchment paper to separate the patties and store in an airtight container. Allow them to chill in the refrigerator for at least 30 minutes. The dough needs to be cold enough that it holds together when you form your Barnburner.

3  When you're ready to serve, warm a large skillet over medium heat. You'll want to have your pan prepared as soon as you have your Barnburner formed. The pan needs to be hot enough to get a sear on the outside quickly; you don't want to wait too long for the Barnburner to heat up, allowing the ice cream inside to melt in the process. Lay a scoop of your ice cream in the center of one of the patties, and then lay the second patty over the top. Using your fingers, press together the top and bottom around the scoop, forming an insulated pouch.

4  Set your Barnburner on the skillet and sear it for 8 to 10 seconds on each side, or until your home is filled with the irresistible aroma of freshly baked cookies and the crust is golden brown.

5  Serve immediately, and go forth into a world in which dessert will never be the same.

## SUGGESTED RIFF

**RICE KRISPIES TREAT BARNBURNER:** The chewy pliability of classic Rice Krispies Treats makes these exceptionally well suited to becoming a Barnburner "shell." First make a sheet of thin treats, and then cut them into squares. You can sandwich a scoop of ice cream between two layers and pinch the edges closed. Their intrinsic stickiness ensures a secure closure. Follow the skillet instructions as for the cookie dough version to toast to perfection.

# BARN-BLOOPERS TURNED TOASTY ICE CREAM SANDWICHES

These have been some Barnburner experiments that, while not quite structurally sound, still turned out totally delicious.

## PB&J

There are two schools of thought on the construction here: The original version of this was a beast, begun by crafting two peanut butter and jelly sandwiches—two full versions, each with two slices of bread and the standard PB&J interior. Next, a scoop of ice cream was laid on top of one sandwich, before being sandwiched by the second sandwich (you follow me?). Which makes this a double-decker, peanut-butter-and-jelly sandwich sandwich.

The slightly less intense option is to apply a slather of peanut butter to one sturdy slice of bread (standard white bread is not quite hardy enough to hold up to this application). On a separate slice of bread, spread your jelly selection. In between, introduce your ice cream of choice. Flatten the scoop gently so that the bread can close around it.

The PB&J can be served at room temperature, but I like to quickly give it a spin in the skillet for a toasty, creamy take on America's favorite lunchbox staple.

## COCONUT-LIME STICKY RICE TOASTY ICE CREAM SANDWICH

One afternoon, after ordering from a local Thai spot for lunch, I found myself upending the accompanying container of sticky rice, sacrificing my lunch side in the name of research.

I added a bit of toasted coconut and lime zest to taste, and by forming the sticky rice into balls and then flattening them into patties, I was able to craft slicelike pieces that could function as the "bread" for an ice cream sandwich.

I quickly seared the patties on each side to shore up their construction and served them warm with a scoop sandwiched between. The sticky texture and contrasting temperatures made this a quick favorite, if not a particularly sellable Barnburner execution.

## FRENCH TOAST

A simple sandwich that yields pretty stellar results. Using two slices of French toast as your shell, scoop your choice of ice cream inside. I suggest Oatmeal Cinnamon Ice Cream (page 97) or Bananas Ferrari Ice Cream (page 62).

# CHAPTER 6

# SHAKES, CAKES & SUNDAES

This section is all about ice cream's ambitious side. In these selections, we'll put it on a pedestal, dress it up in its sundae best, and allow it to indulge in a luxurious milk bath. Each recipe is an opportunity for ice cream to accessorize and hit the town—for a special occasion, a celebration, or simply because we feel like it.

## SHAKES

THE PUMPKIN PIE SHAKE 189

EVERYTHING BAGEL SHAKE
WITH MALTED BARLEY SYRUP &
CREAM CHEESE 191

OLIVE OIL & VANILLA LIME
MILKSHAKE 192

## SUNDAES

ROMAN HONEYMOON: AN
ICE CREAM CHEESE PLATE 200

TENNESSEE BBQ SUNDAE 201

HOW MANY TIMES MUST I SAY
ICE CREAM FOR BREAKFAST?
SUNDAE 202

## ICE CREAM CAKES

MARGARITA CAKE 194

CHOCOLATE CHIP COOKIE
DOUGH CAKE 195

WHIFFER NUTTER EN FUEGO
CAKE 197

I PAVLOVA ICE CREAM CAKE 198

# SHAKES

AS OLD SCHOOL AS IT GETS, milkshakes have long been diner staples and roadside refreshments. But there's more to sample than strictly vanilla, chocolate, and strawberry varieties. These drinkable desserts are inspired by all manner of meals and memories and make perfect portable treats for those seeking something sweet to-go.

# THE PUMPKIN PIE
SERVES 1 SHAKE

When I was in high school, the idea of work was thrilling to me. To serve people, to be behind a counter somewhere, to restock shelves, or to make something that someone else would *pay* for—it was all so glamorous!

As soon as I legally could, I went and got myself two jobs, one in a local bakery. It was in that kitchen that I became hooked on all things culinary.

My first real revelation was pumpkin pie. I was a picky eater as a child and never tried it when my family would serve it at a holiday table (you *eat* pumpkins?), but when I had my first fresh-from-the-oven slice, I knew I'd found Gourd.

Over the years, pumpkin has become ubiquitous and almost passé, but I think of this as an homage to my teenage desire to multitask—it's pumpkin pie a la mode all in one, and in a convenient travel-ready form!

1 small slice of your favorite pumpkin pie (about $1/8$" thick)

$1^1/_4$ cups ice cream of your choice (I recommend Sage Chocolate Chip Ice Cream, page 58, or Salty Buttered Honey Ice Cream, page 80)

2–4 tablespoons whole milk

1. In a blender, or in a bowl using an immersion blender, thoroughly blend the pie, ice cream, and 2 tablespoons of the milk. If you prefer a super-thick shake, you are done. If it's too thick for your taste, add a bit more milk. You can leave your pie pieces a little chunky if you prefer, or keep blending and you'll have a well-integrated and velvety glass of gourd-y goodness.

2. I like to serve this shake in a mason jar with an old-school striped straw and tons of whipped cream, but to be honest, it'd be just as delicious out of a paper bag.

# EVERYTHING BAGEL SHAKE
## WITH MALTED BARLEY SYRUP
## & CREAM CHEESE SERVES 1

How I married someone who doesn't like ice cream is still beyond me. I guess I just figured I'd marry her first and try to change her later.

To that point, I often try to transform things she loves into sweets, thus cheating the system and cleverly redirecting her cravings. And there are few things she loves more than an everything bagel from a New York deli.

According to the foremost authorities, malted barley syrup is the secret weapon without which the great bagels of the world would cease to exist. Who am I to argue?

1 cup Blank Ice Cream Base (page 54)
$\frac{1}{4}$ teaspoon sesame seeds
$\frac{1}{4}$ teaspoon poppy seeds
1 teaspoon dried minced onion
1 tablespoon cream cheese
2 tablespoons whole milk
1 tablespoon malted barley syrup
Bagel chip, for garnish

In a blender, or in a bowl using an immersion blender, thoroughly blend the blank base, seeds, onion, cream cheese, milk, and barley syrup. Serve in a milkshake glass with a bagel chip garnish.

# OLIVE OIL & VANILLA LIME

SERVES 1  *MILKSHAKE*

Sometimes a massage is the perfect escape. At other times, it can be downright delicious. This flavor is inspired by a specific spa experience in which, for 60 minutes, I was basted generously with a combination of extra virgin olive oil and essence of lime. And let me tell you, I have never left a massage so hungry in my life.

Olive oils love citrus (can't say I blame them), and in milkshake form, a little bit of good-quality, fruity oil contributes an extra-lush and creamy character. Lemon and grapefruit are great in this recipe, too, but there's something about the love between the sweet, bright oil and the sour lime that outshines its citrusy siblings.

This shake is also great with a sprinkle of cinnamon and a handful of crushed almonds or toasted coconut. Sip it, scoop it, or—I can honestly say—go ahead and *bathe* in it.

1 cup Blank Ice Cream Base (page 54)
1 tablespoon good-quality olive oil
2 tablespoons whole milk
1 tablespoon lime zest
1 tablespoon lime juice
Seeds scraped from 1 vanilla bean

In a blender, or in a bowl using an immersion blender, thoroughly blend the blank base, oil, milk, lime zest, lime juice, and vanilla bean seeds. Serve in a milkshake glass with a twist of lime and Sea-Salted Whip (page 45).

# ICE CREAM CAKES

WE'VE ADEQUATELY EXPLORED WHY ice cream itself is special, but this takes the cake (sorry, I couldn't resist). The kids who came to school with cupcakes had nothing on those who showed up with layers of creamy cold goodness.

I was one of the lucky ones. Every year, my mother constructed for me my very own homemade version. We will use the exact same structure here that she used—it isn't groundbreaking, but it is totally satisfying and hugely customizable.

The trick is to have a bit of patience, as you'll need to make sure you freeze these cakes in between building layers. If the ice cream, sauces, or fillings are too warm, they'll churn into one another rather than creating distinct layers.

It's always best if you can use freshly spun ice cream instead of thawing some to spread; however, if logistics and time don't allow, you can prepare ice creams ahead of time and allow them to soften slightly—just enough to be spreadable—before working them into your layers.

# MARGARITA CAKE

Commercially made sour mix finds its way into all manner of cabana-side cocktails, and the whole affair makes me so very sad. Why ruin a perfectly good tequila with a syrupy, chemical-laden, and cloyingly sweet liquid?

This cake gives you the best of the summertime slammer without the headache that comes standard, thanks to sour mix.

### CAKE BASE
**6 cups crushed graham crackers (use a food processor)**

**½ cup butter, melted**

**2 tablespoons agave nectar**

### FILLING
**2 quarts Lemon Bar Ice Cream (page 61)**

**Tequila Lime Curd (page 178)**

**Sea-Salted Whip (page 45)**

1. **To make the cake base:** Preheat the oven to 350°F. Grease a 9″ springform pan.

2. In a medium bowl, stir the cracker crumbs, butter, and agave nectar together until well integrated. Press into the pan, using your fingers. Bake for 10 minutes and allow to cool completely.

3. **To fill:** Once the crust is cooled completely, begin layering in the filling. Spread the first quart of Lemon Bar over the surface of the crust and return to the freezer for 20 to 30 minutes, or until firm. Once fully chilled, spread a layer of Tequila Lime Curd and again return the cake to the freezer for about 10 minutes, or until the curd is firm. (If the curd is too warm, it will churn into the ice cream rather than remain a distinct layer.)

4. Once the curd is firm, remove the cake from the freezer and spread the final quart of Lemon Bar Ice Cream evenly across the surface. Return to the freezer until prepared to serve.

5. Just before serving, remove the cake from the freezer and release the sides of the pan. Using an offset spatula, spread Sea-Salted Whip over the top of the cake. You can double the recipe for the whip and also frost the sides of the cake, if you'd prefer.

6. Slice and serve.

# CHOCOLATE CHIP
**SERVES 20 TO 24** *COOKIE DOUGH CAKE*

I f we put chunks of the stuff in our ice cream, it stands to reason that it'd be just as enjoyable holding it up. Using the eggless cookie dough recipe from the Barnburner application, this cake is chocolate chip cookie dough ice cream on steroids. If I can make a recommendation here, I suggest the following construction: 1 quart Grape-Nuts Ice Cream (page 96), Honeyed Peanut Butter Sauce (page 25), 1 quart Salty Buttered Honey Ice Cream (page 80), Malted Hot Fudge (page 35), Sea-Salted Chocolate-Covered Pecan Toffee (page 18), and Sea-Salted Whip (page 45).

**Chocolate Chip Cookie Dough Barnburner (page 181), minus the ice cream**

**2 sauces of your choice**

**2 quarts ice cream of your choice, softened before use**

**Topping of your choice**

**Whip of your choice**

1 Once the dough has been mixed, press it into a 9″ springform pan to form the base of the cake. Spread the first sauce over the cookie surface and refrigerate for 15 to 30 minutes, or until firm. Remove from the freezer and spread the first quart of softened ice cream over the surface.

2 Return to the freezer for 15 to 30 minutes, or until firm. Once set, remove from the freezer and spread with the second sauce. Into the still-liquid sauce, sprinkle topping. Return to the freezer for another 15 to 30 minutes, or until firm.

3 Once the middle sauce and topping layer have set, remove the cake from the freezer and spread the second softened quart of ice cream over the surface. Return to the freezer for at least 15 to 30 minutes.

4 Just before serving, remove the cake from the freezer and remove the sides of the pan. Using an offset spatula, spread the whip over the top of the cake. (You can also double the recipe for the whip and frost all sides of the cake, if you prefer.)

5 Slice and serve.

# WHIFFER NUTTER

SERVES 20 TO 24 *EN FUEGO CAKE*

Equal parts satisfaction and showmanship, this makes a great birthday cake—you won't even need to buy candles.

## CAKE BASE

3 cups crushed chocolate pebble cereal (use a food processor)

1/2 cup butter, melted

2 tablespoons peanut butter

## FILLING

1 quart Bananas Ferrari Ice Cream (page 62)

1 quart Honeyed Peanut Butter Sauce (page 25)

1 1/2 cups Salty Buttered Honey Ice Cream (page 80)

1 recipe of Marshmallow Whiff (page 36)

1. **To make the cake base:** Preheat the oven to 350°F. Grease a 9" springform pan.

2. In a medium bowl, stir together the cereal crumbs, butter, and peanut butter until well integrated. Press into the pan, using your fingers. Bake for 10 minutes and allow to cool completely.

3. **To fill:** Once the crust is cooled completely, begin layering. Spread the Bananas Ferrari layer and return the cake to the freezer for 20 to 30 minutes, or until firm. Remove from the freezer and spread the Honeyed Peanut Butter Sauce over the ice cream. Return to the freezer for 10 to 15 minutes, or until the sauce has hardened slightly. Spread the Salty Buttered Honey Ice Cream and return to the freezer for another 20 to 30 minutes, or until firm.

4. Once the cake is ready to serve, remove it from the freezer and, using an offset spatula, spread the Marshmallow Whiff over the top. It will be sticky and a bit tricky to work with; keep a cup of warm water nearby into which you can dip the spatula to help the process.

5. Using a kitchen torch and working quickly and carefully, heat the surface of the whiff with the flame. Once torched to perfection, serve immediately!

# I PAVLOVA
*ICE CREAM CAKE*

I lived an embarrassingly extended period of time assuming that the name of this ethereal dessert and the Russian ballerina had no relation. Once I realized the error, I began to idolize Anna Pavlova—but not because of her dancing prowess. No, I want to be Anna Pavlova because how many contemporary figures can say they've had a bona fide dessert named after them?

This airy meringue-based cake, with its slightly crisp shell and chewy center, also provides the perfect pedestal. Texturally, it offers distinction from the ice cream without a dramatic interruption of the eating experience. I suggest the following construction over your Pavlova base: Salty Buttered Honey Ice Cream (page 80), Quick Pickled Berries (page 40), and Sea-Salted Whip (page 45).

## PAVLOVA

6 egg whites

Pinch of salt

2 cups superfine sugar

1 teaspoon balsamic vinegar

3 tablespoons unsweetened cocoa powder

2 ounces semisweet chocolate, finely chopped

## CAKE

1 quart ice cream of your choice, softened before use

Topping of your choice

Whip of your choice

1. **To make the Pavlova:** Preheat the oven to 300°F and grease a 9″ springform pan.

2. In the bowl of a stand mixer, combine the egg whites and salt. Using the whisk attachment, beat until soft peaks form. Add the sugar gradually and continue beating.

3. Once the peaks are stiff and shiny, add the vinegar. Sprinkle in the cocoa and chocolate and gently fold everything together.

4. Spread the meringue evenly and to the edges of the springform pan. Bake for 60 to 70 minutes, or until the meringue is firm but still somewhat soft in the center. Remove from the oven and allow to cool completely.

5. **To make the cake:** Once the Pavlova has cooled, spread the ice cream over it and return the cake to the freezer for 20 to 30 minutes, or until firm. Once set, remove from the freezer and layer on the topping. Freeze until ready to serve. Just before serving, remove the cake from the freezer and remove the sides of the pan. Using an offset spatula, spread the whip over the top of the cake. (You can also double the recipe for the whip and frost all sides of the cake, if you prefer.)

# SUNDAES

*SO MANY SUNDAES START* with good intentions but result in an unfortunate and clashing puddle of incompatible, discordant dregs.

It may not be rocket science, but the construction of a sundae does need to acknowledge a few critical components: flavor combinations, temperatures, textures, and, ultimately, the agreeability of ingredients. A really stellar ice cream sundae is one that has sturdy blueprints drawn up, with proper consideration paid to the start-to-finish experience.

Particularly with lesser-known flavors like the ones in this book, there is some understandable apprehension when attempting to match multiple options.

# ROMAN HONEYMOON: SERVES 2
## AN ICE CREAM CHEESE PLATE

With three cheese-based flavors and all the necessary accoutrements, this sundae eats like a perfectly laid-out cheese selection.

1 scoop Feta Tomato Swirl Ice Cream (page 78)

1 scoop *Finocchio e la Capra* Ice Cream (page 76)

1 scoop *Cacio e Pepe* Ice Cream (page 83)

2 tablespoons good-quality honey

1 teaspoon olive oil

1 tablespoon toasted bread crumbs

1 teaspoon lemon zest

Sea-Salted Whip (page 45)

1 On a serving plate, arrange the 3 ice cream scoops in a triangle. Drizzle evenly with the honey and oil and sprinkle with the bread crumbs and lemon zest, reserving a pinch of each.

2 Dollop with Sea-Salted Whip. Sprinkle with the remaining lemon zest and bread crumbs and serve.

# TENNESSEE BBQ

SERVES 1 *SUNDAE*

Sure, it may sound a little strange, but this is the dessert of pulled pork sandwiches: the warm and savory pork and the pillowy biscuit, the tartness of the pickled berries cutting through the entire dish, contributing the acidic punch required to brighten and contrast with the rest of this rich composition. Just trust me on this one.

1 Better-Than-Buttermilk Biscuit (page 132)

¾ cup Caramel Ice Cream Braised Pork Shoulder (page 152)

2 tablespoons Quick Pickled Berries (page 40)

1 scoop Brown Sugar BBQ Softer-Serve (page 118)

Sea-Salted Whip (page 45), optional

1 This recipe is best when the biscuits are a bit warm. If they're not fresh from the oven, cut them in half and toast lightly in a skillet.

2 I like to build this sundae from the bottom up. In a sundae dish, first place the bottom half of the biscuit, then a layer of pork, followed by a dressing of pickled berries (this will act as a buffer between the warm pork and cold ice cream). Next add a scoop of Brown Sugar BBQ, and then complete the sundae with a biscuit top. A dollop of Sea Salted Whip on the side never hurt anyone, either.

3 Serve immediately and forget the rules.

# HOW MANY TIMES MUST I SAY
# ICE CREAM FOR BREAKFAST?

SERVES 1 OR 2 *SUNDAE*

Do I need to explain?

1 slice Melted Ice Cream French Toast
(page 136)

1 scoop Bananas Ferrari Ice Cream
(page 62)

1 scoop Doughnut Ya Love Coffee Ice Cream
(page 94)

2 tablespoons Coffee Caramel Sauce
(page 30)

Sea-Salted Whip (page 45)

Malted Salted Toffee (page 21)

While still warm, set the French toast in a dish. Top with the 2 ice cream scoops, arranged side by side, and drizzle with the caramel. Dollop on the whip, sprinkle with the toffee, and serve.

# ICE CREAM, GIVE IT A SPIN

As you've probably gathered, there's a big difference between *loving* ice cream and wanting to *make* it. In fact, one of the things that I love about making it is that it is something very few people attempt to do. There's something about making a pan of brownies or a tray of cookies that feels comfortable to folks at home. They've seen their grandmothers do it; they've used that iconic red Betty Crocker box mix to make an artificially colored, sunshine-yellow, fancifully frosted birthday cake. There's nothing too mysterious about that process.

I don't remember the first time I made ice cream at home or what motivated me. The outcome was obviously very forgettable. In fact, probably the first dozen or so attempts were forgettable (perhaps even repressed). I don't know what flavors I attempted or where the recipes came from. I know that I owned my little red Cuisinart for a very long time before I even liberated it from its cardboard box.

I do, however, remember the circumstances in which I received the machine. It was the holiday season, and I was spending the majority of my time perusing catalogues, clicking through e-mails, eagerly eating up whatever Williams-Sonoma happened to be pitching at that time.

It was in one such sponsored e-mail that I first saw her: In Santa Claus–suit red was a jolly-looking little ice cream maker. There was even a gift bundle in which she was accompanied by festive jars of hot fudge and seasonally hued sprinkles. I had never owned an ice cream maker—I wasn't even sure I wanted to make ice cream—but something

about that holiday spirit made me hit the ever-so-subtle "Send a Wish List" link.

I typed something along the lines of "A fun project for the new year?" then filled in my mother's e-mail address and clicked the diminutive digital paper plane. I didn't think much of it again until the morning of December 25th. All of the gifts had been disrobed of their convivial dressings. One box remained behind the tree, and as the detritus of another successful Noel was being swept up by my father, Rosie approached me with that final package.

I was thrilled, of course, and I welcomed Red into my home with good intentions. But in post-holiday efforts to tidy up, she was stashed on top of the refrigerator for later use. There she lived for several subsequent years, snug in her Styrofoam, separated from her hot fudge and sprinkle buddies, who were given a home in the hospitable pantry and enjoyed in a far more timely fashion.

Perhaps it was intimidation at being indoctrinated into the ice-cream-making fold. Or perhaps I hesitated out of concern that I could damage the experience, lose a little of what made ice cream so special by lifting the veil. It'd be like going behind the scenes in Disney World; I wasn't so sure I wanted to know where Mickey Mouse took his cheese break, if you feel me.

And while I don't remember the circumstances, I eventually unboxed the spinner and unstuck myself from whatever was keeping us apart. Intermittently I'd fall into spells in which I'd churn through half a dozen batches, then return Red to her cardboard crib, and my ice cream itch would again go dormant.

Each time I returned to the practice, though, I did so with renewed vigor,

glamorizing the most recent batch, even if in reality it had wound up a mass of wobbly goo or some barely edible iteration of a flat flavor.

There's something enchanting about the challenge. There's a romance to the reticence with which we approach this practice. And as with all great risks, the reward is that much sweeter for the string of inevitable failures.

I don't know how many people have had the good fortune of tasting fresh ice cream out of a freezer, but there is simply nothing like it. For all of the hassle that making ice cream can be, for the headaches and the heartbreak and—if you're like me—the tears through which we watch perfectly selected ingredients make an untimely trip down the drain, when the stars align, the result is worth every bad batch.

It's my hope that this book has helped you to find the confidence and inspiration to create these memories for yourself and your friends and family. To make your ice cream your own and share it with the people you love. After all, it's like serving them a tiny frozen scoop of your soul.

And despite now having owned a stable of ice cream spinners, from countertop Cadillacs to commercial-grade, 1,200-pound behemoths capable of pushing out massive quantities at pulse-racing speeds, I still have old Red. She's been moved around a lot, but the old girl still gives me her best.

I've finally managed to give her a more comfortable place to stay: a cozy cabinet all her own. It's still above the refrigerator, but these days she's totally out of the box.

# THANK YOU.

Mollie Glick, for being a serious ice cream fan—and also for being a friend, for seeing something in me and for supporting me from day one.

Dervla Kelly, for freedom, advice and encouragement—and for generally making me sound good.

Rae Ann Spitzenberger, for your vision in creating a book that I can be so proud of.

Lisa Homa & Cindi Gasparre, for slogging through a sugar-soaked photo shoot with style. I owe you both something savory.

Tina Rupp, for bringing recipes to life with stunning photography—and understanding the value of a solid doughnut.

Stephanie Hanes, for knowing how critical the details can be.

Joy Fowlkes, for facilitating communication and sharing food articles for me to geek out on.

Rosie, for being my best friend. What more can I say?

Kev, for always providing structure—be it physical framework or familial. You're my rock.

Nonnie & Grandpa, for showing me handcrafted—long before the term was hip—with homemade spaghetti and wine. And for always being so proud of me.

Linda Albanese, for showing me that a mother-in-law can make a truly great friend.

The Albanese clan, for warm welcomes and so much laughter around the dinner table. And for Grandpa's gravy to balance out the mountains of sugar in my life.

Farrin Jacobs, where would I be without your expert palate, editing skills, and exceptional packaging prowess? From Prime Meats for cocktails to lugging that ridiculous sign halfway across town. Always above and beyond, friend. I owe you ice cream for life.

Chrissy Ward, for taking a leap of faith, loving Christmas so fiercely, and being an inimitable culinarian. This book would not have been possible without your exceptional skill.

Jeremy Arkin, for turning one wild summer totally upside down with me. Promise to always bring Batman to job interviews.

Antonio Diaz, for keeping me on track, being so generous with support and friendship, inspiring me to be a better writer and a better person.

Gia Hughes, for being a sounding board and a friend. The next book'll be a vegan one.

Lindsay Carroll, for the countless DQ runs in high school—for being there for literally *everything* in my life. I love you!

Patrick & Rachel Rue, for showing me how to create flavor, think outside the box, and run a business, and most of all, for demonstrating the importance of being friendly and kind.

Jarred & Ashley, Jonas & Lauryn, Evan & Aubrey, for being there during those formative years.

Carrie Agin, from lab partners to brunch buddies, I value your opinions and friendship—and your french fries.

Cristina Sciarra, the bonds forged during ice cream college are frozen in time.

Diana Hardeman, for being a kindred spirit.

Emily. I'd hardly have ever put pen to paper in my life if you hadn't seen something in me, encouraged me, animated me, and supported me in every crazy thing I've come up with. Your patience, sacrifice, and understanding throughout this madness make you a saint. Your imagination, gumption, and generosity establishes you the most influential, inspiring person in my life. You make every day an adventure; I couldn't consider myself luckier to have you as my teammate. Snack cakes are just better together.

# INDEX

Underscored page references indicate sidebar text or tips. **Boldfaced** page references indicate photographs.